TAMING TIME
A PRACTICAL GUIDE TO TIME MANAGEMENT

PN 9170417 0

CHANDOS BUSINESS GUIDES
BUSINESS SKILLS

Chandos Business Guides are designed to provide managers with practical, down-to-earth information. The Chandos Business Guides are written by leading authors in their respective fields. If you would like to receive a full listing of current and forthcoming titles, please visit our web site www.chandospublishing.com or contact Melinda Taylor on email mtaylor@chandospublishing.com or direct telephone number +44 (0) 1865 882727.

New authors: we are always pleased to receive ideas for new titles; if you would like to write a Chandos Business Guide, please contact Dr Glyn Jones on email gjones@chandospublishing.com or direct telephone number +44 (0) 1865 884447.

Bulk orders: some organisations buy a number of copies of our books. If you are interested in doing this, we would be pleased to discuss a discount. Please contact Dr Glyn Jones on email gjones@chandospublishing.com or direct telephone number +44 (0) 1865 884447.

TAMING TIME
A PRACTICAL GUIDE TO TIME MANAGEMENT

RICHARD MOXHAM

Chandos Publishing
Oxford · England

Chandos Publishing (Oxford) Limited
Chandos House
5 & 6 Steadys Lane
Stanton Harcourt
Oxford OX8 1RL
England
Tel: +44 (0) 1865 882727 Fax: +44 (0) 1865 884448
Email: sales@chandospublishing.com
www.chandospublishing.com

First published in Great Britain in 2001

ISBN 1 902375 73 4

© R. Moxham, 2001

All rights reserved. No part of this publication may be reproduced, stored in or introduced into a retrieval system, or transmitted, in any form, or by any means (electronic, mechanical, photocopying, recording or otherwise) without the prior written permission of the Publishers. This publication may not be lent, resold, hired out or otherwise disposed of by way of trade in any form of binding or cover other than that in which it is published without the prior consent of the Publishers. Any person who does any unauthorised act in relation to this publication may be liable to criminal prosecution and civil claims for damages.

The Publishers make no representation, express or implied, with regard to the accuracy of the information contained in this publication and cannot accept any legal responsibility or liability for any errors or omissions.

The material contained in this publication constitutes general guidelines only and does not represent to be advice on any particular matter. No reader or purchaser should act on the basis of material contained in this publication without first taking professional advice appropriate to their particular circumstances. Readers of this publication should be aware that only Acts of Parliament and Statutory Instruments have the force of law and that only courts can authoritatively interpret the law.

Printed by Biddles, Guildford, UK

Contents

Acknowledgements ix

Introduction xi

About the author xix

PART 1 STEPPING BACK

1 Setting the context – life not work 3

2 Principles and values 11

3 Introducing the three-point model 25

    Stepping back – key messages and action plan 31

PART 2 GETTING FOCUSED

4 Why am I here? 37

5 Thinking smart 41

6	The three time frames	45
	Getting focused – key messages and action plan	49

PART 3 GETTING ORGANISED

7	Putting order into chaos	55
8	Prioritising	65
9	Systems and discipline	79
10	Why plan if it will all change anyway?	93
	Getting organised – key messages and action plan	97

PART 4 STAYING FOCUSED

11	So why does it all go wrong?	103
12	Behaviour and communication	109
	Staying focused – key messages and action plan	125

PART 5 SPECIFIC TIME MANAGEMENT TECHNIQUES

13	Be in tune with your body	133
14	Delegating	141
15	The meetings myth	155

16	Think 'team'	167
17	The e-world issues	175
18	Be decisive – go for the hard tasks	199
19	Task batching	203
20	'No interrupt' zones	209
21	Realistic time estimation	215
22	Travel and away time	221
23	Be creative as well as corrective	227
24	Managing stress	231
	Specific time management techniques – key messages and action plan	241

PART 6 THE BEGINNING

| 25 | Where do you go from here? | 251 |

Acknowledgements

One of my ambitions has always been to write a book. When Glyn Jones of Chandos approached me about this project I faced a dilemma. Yes it was the opportunity I always wanted; however, my concern, ironically given the subject of the book, was I doubted that I had enough time to devote to the project. I see myself as a busy person. Without the encouragement and cajoling of my wife, Susan, I would probably not have committed to the project.

During many years as a training consultant I have met hundreds of people who have been participants on workshops I have facilitated. These workshops covered a number of business skills, often including time management. I believe that I learned something from each of those workshops. From discussions and the sharing of experiences, on each occasion I walked away with some new perspectives, fresh ideas and additional answers. I hope that the participants learned as well, but I have never had the view that as a training facilitator I had all of the answers. So my thanks to the many, who have unknowingly contributed to this book.

I am indebted to my colleagues at hr Team. They supported me in this work and recognised that writing this book was an important project for me. They never complained that I was spending too much time on this personal 'mission'; I hope I was not. If I did, I am grateful that they understood and never complained.

Finally my thanks to the clients who, over the years, have asked me to develop time management programmes for their organisations. The thinking and the research that these projects involved helped me develop the concepts and ideas for what has become *Taming Time*.

Introduction

This book is for *busy people* – people who feel that there are too many things to do in the time available. Taking the decision to read this book is therefore an additional pressure as it involves taking time from an already hectic schedule of tasks and meetings, and business and private commitments.

I hope that when you have completed your reading you will feel that the investment in time has been worthwhile. I am confident that you will then be more able to manage your time more effectively, will feel more in control and will suffer less stress from time pressures. Investment is a theme throughout the book. You will need to invest time to make more time in the future. Sometimes the investment will feel like an act of faith, as you will be feeling that what I am suggesting will encroach even more on that limited resource, time. Suspend judgement, as the investment will provide you with the payback of more discretionary time in the future.

Consider the following three points.

Paradox one

In an age where there is legislation that protects people from having to work excessive hours why is it that more and more people are working longer and longer hours? The UK, with its relatively unregulated labour laws, is now seen as the sweatshop of the first world economies, but my experience is that in continental Europe and the US people are also experiencing longer working hours.

Paradox two

While there is an increasing range of time management systems available – be they paper or electronic based – the level of chaos grows. How many times have you attended meetings where people diligently record actions, agreements and commitments in those systems? How many times have the deadlines subsequently come and gone? How many times have you experienced inaction? How many times have you felt, as I have, that the meeting, the commitments were illusions – frankly, that it was all a dream?

Paradox three

Do you believe that a significant proportion of the population have a death wish? It is now widely recognised that too heavy a workload leads to stress. Stress-related illness is one of the early twenty-first century ailments. Many corporations are now so concerned that they have introduced stress reduction programmes. Yet, in spite of this awareness, why do so many people push themselves to the limit? They commit to manic schedules of meetings and over-ambitious deadlines, and take on more and more responsibilities.

Should we be surprised by any of this? I do not think so!

Businesses move at an increasingly frenetic pace. Technological change and intensive global competition mean that whereas strategy change used to be measured in months and years it is now seen in terms of days and weeks. Remember the old adage that a week is a long time in politics? In the IT market sector, where I have spent a lot of my business life, the changes in a week equate to three years in the 'old economy'!

Businesses have been delayered and flattened. The 'doers' now provide their own support systems. Largely the days where people have the luxury of secretaries, resources to 'protect' them from the day-to-day realities, have long gone. Communication tools – the mobile phone, e-mail – mean that there are no hiding places left.

All of these factors build up time pressures, not just in terms of absolute workload, but in the immediacy of communication and the expectation of a rapid response.

Let us return to Paradox 2, the availability of more – and more clever – time systems. Having a system is important, an essential element of effective time management. I will cover systems in detail in Part 4 of this book. However, a system on its own is not the answer. A system is a support tool, but to achieve effective management of time requires something much deeper.

I have outlined some of the issues. Clearly managing time is not easy! I appreciate that you have purchased this book to get answers, which I will attempt to provide. However, first I must manage your expectations. *There are no wonder cures, no magic solutions.* Would you believe me if I said there were? If there were any single answer to the perennial problem of time someone would have found it by now.

I hope that this outbreak of honesty will not tempt you to put the book down and right its purchase off as a bad investment. There are answers, but no single solution. Being effective at managing time involves improving and changing a number of things. The combined effects will give you results.

This book is designed to provide you with inputs and perspectives on each of the elements that will contribute to more effective time management. It is a *practical guide*, from which you can take ideas and suggestions for immediate action. It assumes the real world, not an ideal world.

As you work through the book something will quickly become evident. That is that effective time management involves a lot more than time management 'techniques'. I am not deriding techniques – indeed a whole section of the book is devoted to them. However, to become more effective at managing time requires a lot more than technique. I will therefore be setting techniques in the context of these other important elements.

This book is organised in six parts, following a logical structure that takes you from concepts through to specific time management action and techniques.

- **Part 1**, 'Stepping back', looks at the subject at a conceptual level. It introduces a three-point model, which provides a framework for thinking effective use of time, and also drives the structure of the book.

- **Part 2**, 'Getting focused', challenges the trap of 'what do I need to do in the time available? It introduces a different perspective – 'what can I achieve in the time available?"'

- **Part 3**, 'Getting organised', is a logical follow-on from getting focused. Once there is focus on achievement, the next stage is to be organised in such a way that activities are directed to the achievement of the defined goals.

- **Part 4**, 'Staying focused', looks at a range of skills not usually associated with time management. You can have the most focused plans, the most comprehensive time management systems, but without the behavioural skills to enable you to manage people and communications you will not become an effective time manager.

- **Part 5,** 'Specific time management techniques', deals with what I have already said that, on their own, will not make effective time managers. However, they are essential ingredients. In this part we will discuss a range of techniques, set in the context of new organisational structures and the 'e world'.

- **Part 6**, the final part of the book, is entitled 'The beginning'. By now you will, I hope, have discovered a number of new ideas, principles and techniques that will help you manage your time more effectively in the future. However, if, when you put this book down you say to yourself 'that was interesting' then carry on as before, nothing will change. Completing the book is the start of the road to more effective time management. This final part provides you with some guidelines for putting together your own action plan. Yes, this will take time, but remember the principle that you need to invest time to make time.

To help you retain what you have learned as you work through the book and to log the most relevant points for you there is a section at the end of each part for you to complete before you move on to the next topic. Take the time to do this, as these notes will help you formulate your action plan.

To complete the introduction let me leave you with two thoughts that may be the starting point to a change of thinking about time and time management. Remember that effective time management is as much about mindset as about techniques.

Firstly, the entire label 'time management' is incorrect. You cannot actually manage time! It is a resource that quietly ticks away – once used it has gone forever. It is a non-reusable resource. How long have you spent reading this introduction? You cannot now reverse the decision and use that time again to do something else. So, you cannot manage time. However, you *can manage what you want to achieve* in the time available. This may be a subtle definition, but it is an important one.

Secondly, do you see time as an enemy? I think that many people do. 'Where does the time go?' 'There are not enough hours in the day.' 'Everything takes longer than I had planned.' You see? Time is seen as a battle. Time – or lack of it – is seen as the demon. Consider changing your perspective – think of time as a resource. If you *tame time* you can start to use that resource effectively.

About the author

Richard Moxham has had many years' business experience having held top-level positions in sales and marketing at major companies including A.C. Nielsen, Proctor & Gamble, the Xerox Corporation and Lex plc.

Richard has now been a training consultant for 15 years and is a senior consultant in the UK operation of hr TEAM, a Europe-wide training consultancy specialising in personal development, leadership, management, team development, sales and business skills. Since moving into training consultancy he has developed and facilitated time management programmes for a number of well known major companies, and has gained a wealth of experience working for international firms from the USA and mainland Europe as well as the UK, including General Motors, Cable & Wireless Communications, Lotus Development Corporation, Unisys, BMW, Axa, AT&T, Sun Microsystems and Esselte. Richard has also recently been awarded the status of accredited time management facilitator for Time/system.

The author may be contacted at:

> hr TEAM UK Ltd
>
> Ash House
>
> Station Road
>
> HEATHFIELD
>
> East Sussex
>
> TN21 8LD
>
> Tel: 01435 865711
>
> Fax: 01435 865933
>
> E-mail: richard.moxham@hrteam.co.uk
>
> Web: www.hrteam.co.uk

PART 1

Stepping back

CHAPTER 1

Setting the context – life not work

Why balance in and out of work time?

Making plans, and managing your time at a life and not just a work level is one of the principles of effective time management. It is also a prerequisite for leading a full and rewarding life! Time management training courses and books on the subject have been available for many years. In the main they have focused on managing time at work. I am not preaching anarchy here, suggesting that you turn your back on work and concentrate on leisure. I am suggesting that placing equal importance on planning your 'in work' and 'out of work' time will benefit you, your business if you are a business owner, or your employer.

This does not mean that every minute of your out of work time has to be planned and allocated down to the last 15 minutes. It is perfectly acceptable, and in fact beneficial to, at times, do nothing. In our society the active lifestyle is promoted. The achiever at work is the achiever in leisure. My feeling is that an active lifestyle is better than that of a couch potato, but you have the right to decide to do nothing! I make this point to dispel any fears you may have about a life where all of your time, in and out of work, is allocated and filled with planned activities.

What is important? An awareness of the benefits to you, your work, your friends and your family of achieving the balance of rewarding, enjoyable and fulfilling in and out of work time.

How many hours do I have?

There may be a notional average working week, but if you asked twenty people how many hours they work you will probably get twenty different answers. My guess is that most people work longer than the stated national average, so for the sake of this exercise I will take an average of 45 hours. Let me assure you that this book is not full of mathematical calculations. In fact the ones you are about to see are the only ones in the entire work. I could cut out the numbers and make the simple statement that most of us only focus on, in planning terms, a relatively small percentage of the total time we have available. However, I don't think that the majority of you would believe me. Hence, I am resorting to science to prove my case.

- In a year there are 8,736 hours.

- Assuming you are working for 48 weeks of the year, then your total annual working hours are 2,160.

- How many hours a day do you sleep? We will take an average eight hours, which comes to 2,920 hours per year.

- This leaves you with 3,656 hours per year, or, on average, 70 hours per week when you are not working or sleeping.

So, what is the point of the exercise? Firstly, most of us tend to try to plan, organise and manage our work time, which accounts for 37% of our available time. I have taken sleep time out of the equation, but of course the high-energy individuals among you who can get by on four hours per night will have to make another calculation. Coming back to the 'average' person, waking non-work time represents around 63% of the total. Question – why do so many people focus on the 37%, while spending relatively little time thinking about or making the most of the 63%? I have met so many people in business who appear to work to the rule of 'out of work time is the bit left over when the work commitments have been met'. This cannot be right for them, their employers or their family. Of course, we all face times when we have to work that bit harder, commit that bit more time. This is fine, but it is a different situation to a norm of work always taking priority. If you are now questioning the calculation on the basis that you are not in the 45-hour working week average and that you are working, say, a 70-hour week, then please recognise the red flag! Read on.

Living to work, working to live?

Does the following describe the sort of day that you frequently have?

> I tend to get to the office early. I can beat the traffic, and in theory at least I get some space to catch up before the chaos of the day starts. The only problem is that people are now used to me being in early, so I tend to get interruptions earlier and earlier. Nonetheless getting in by 7.45 does give me some opportunity to clear the backlog of e-mails and tidy up what I did not complete the day before.
>
> The standard office hours period – 9.00 through to 5.30 – is generally hectic, filled with a schedule of planned meetings, putting out bush fires and reacting to urgent requests from colleagues, my manager and clients. Often it feels like a survival course, and just having completed it without going backwards can feel like a success. By the time the day starts to wind down I grab the opportunity to action at least some of the things I had intended to do during the day but for some reason failed to do so. Then of course there are the actions I have picked up during the day that I need to slot in somewhere.
>
> By around 6.30 I am endeavouring to make some impact on the inbox of the e-mail system, the contents of which have multiplied during the day. I calculate that if I try to complete everything I should, I will still be in the

office at midnight. So, I throw some papers in my case and pack up the laptop, resigned to doing some catch-up at home after dinner.

Extreme? Believe me it describes the working day of an increasing number of people. In a Quality of Life Working Survey conducted by the Institute of Management and UMIST, 5,000 managers were interviewed; when asked questions relating to working hours and stress, the responses were as follows:

- 10% worked, on average, more than 61 hours per week;
- 33% worked, on average, more than 51 hours per week;
- 82% worked, on average, more than 41 hours per week;
- 71% complained that the length of their working week was having a detrimental effect on their health;
- 79% believed that their work rate was damaging their relationships with their partner and family.

The survey was conducted in 1999. My feeling is that since then the situation is unlikely to have improved. In fact, my belief is that the stresses have increased.

If you can relate to the scenario above, or could well be one of the statistics, then make some commitments to change you work style, and record that commitment at the end of this part of the book. Resisting? Maybe you feel that this pace is good, that it is moral to work these long hours, that you are a model employee? If so move on to the next paragraph and read about *the importance of balance*. Of course, working to live is not the answer either. At the extreme, if you are literally just putting in the hours to receive a pay cheque and the eight hours per day five days a week holds zero interest or motivation, then you are not living, just existing for that percentage of your life. The key is balance.

The importance of balance

I am sure that there are still some companies who see the merit in their employees working over-long hours, believing that they are getting 'value for money'. However, more and more enlightened organisations are introducing work/life initiatives – programmes that are designed to help their people achieve a balance between work, home, leisure and other interests in their lives. These companies are not making this investment totally for altruistic motives. Research in the United States and Europe shows that companies that introduce life/work initiatives see greater commitment, increases in productivity, reduced staff turnover and reduced absenteeism.

Regardless of whether you work for an 'old style' or enlightened employer, or indeed if you are your own employer, you can introduce your own life/work initiative. Taking the learning points from this book can be the first step. You will only commit to such a plan if you buy into the benefits of achieving balance. So, let me summarise what I believe those benefits are:

- You will feel more in control – feeling not in control is one of the major causes of stress.

- You will feel more fulfilled, in that you will be achieving life and family goals as well as those relating to the job.

- You will achieve more at work – remember that achievement is about output, not tasks and activities.

- You will feel better!

We are all different. What represents a heavy, stressful workload for one may be quite comfortable to the next person. Differing private life circumstances will mean that the correct life/work balance will vary person to person. I cannot – and do not wish to – give you a formula. Indeed, there is no fixed model. The key is for you to analyse where you are now, decide where you want to be, and take action to bring about the desired change.

Below are some questions that I would ask you to answer honestly. Those answers will help you define where you are now, how happy you are with 'the now', and therefore what you need to change.

1. How many hours do you typically work in a week?

2. Do you find that level of work time stressful at times?

3. To what extent do you take work home?

4. Do you regularly trade your leisure and family plans to complete commitments?

5. Do your work commitments at times cause conflicts between you and your partner, family and friends?

6. How do you feel most of the time – that you are controlling your work or that your work is controlling you?

7. Do you sometimes feel frustrated with yourself for not being able to get your work/life balance right?

8. When you are drinking a cup of coffee, having a bath or just sitting down taking a break, what are your predominant thoughts – about work or out of work topics?

There is no scoring system, no marks so you can place your scores on a matrix and get instant feedback. The purpose of these questions is to get you thinking about your own situation. You may believe that you have the correct life/work balance. This is fine. You can read the rest of the book with the objective of further developing your effectiveness and productivity. If you feel that you have not got things in balance then read the rest of this book, and consider the guidelines and suggestions in the context of work and out of work, i.e. in *life/work terms*. The principles I will be introducing you to are equally applicable to both elements.

CHAPTER 2

Principles and values

The right mindset

In the Introduction I brought up the notion that effective time management requires a lot more than techniques or skills. Of course they are important, but the beliefs, values and attitudes that you have are fundamental. Being skilled in time management techniques, or using a time management system even on its own, will help, but the inroads you make will be marginal. Having the right attitude, the right beliefs – I will label these the right 'mindset' – is the key to taming time.

One of the mindset blocks is the belief that 'I am the innocent victim'. Time passes, events happen around me, I have no control over this. The view is understandable – I can appreciate why people feel this way. However, I intend to challenge it.

Answer the following questions. Again I would ask you to be honest and objective in your responses – we are not trying to establish a right or a wrong. The objective is to get you thinking about the subject from a different perspective.

1. List out the prime time stealers in your working life – the things that divert you, that events represent interruptions, the incidents that destroy your plans. If you want to, you can extend the question to your whole life, not just your work life. Brainstorm – the list can be as long or as short as you like.

2. Then take a red pen or pencil and underline those over which you believe (and please really question this!) you have absolutely no control.

3. Then take a green pen or pencil and underline those where you believe you have some control. They are in your power to influence, at least to some extent.

4. Then take a blue pen or pencil and underline those over which you are able, if you wish to be, in control.

I have asked these same questions to participants on workshops that I have facilitated. The conclusions are invariably the same:

- Of course there are some events that I have absolutely have no control over, and truthfully never can have. This is realistic, so accept them as a given.

- The greatest debates are around the items where there is some control. These often started in the 'no control category', but after some thought there is the realisation that, yes, I have some influence here – if I choose to!

- The list of factors that I do have control over is generally bigger than I thought it would be.

The outputs from this simple exercise are often the starting point for a change in mindset. I cannot hide behind the innocent victim argument. There are things that I can control. There are things that I can influence. This does not imply a perfect world because there is acknowledgement of the 'no control' items. From this we can focus on where we can make a difference.

The 'Ten Commandments' of time management

Now let us look at the other mindset items. I call the list which follows the *Ten Commandments*, and together they make up the cornerstone of effective time management. They represent the fundamental core values that, if put into practice, will enable you to realign your work methods to achieve more in less time.

1. *I am aware that time is a non-reuseable resource, that I cannot take the last hour back and use it more effectively*

I have already raised this in the Introduction. This does not mean that you should feel pressured about time or become paranoid about this valuable resource slipping away. It is about having a constant awareness that the resource is one-off, and that you can make choices about how to use it. This applies equally to in and out of work time.

2. *I cannot manage time, but I can manage what I achieve within the time available*

Again, this notion has been introduced already. Initially it may seem odd that in a book about time management I am now stating that time cannot be managed. Let me explain. Imagine if you could manage time in the sense of saying: 'Over the next week I will have days of 30 hours because I have a lot to do, a lot to achieve. The following week is less demanding so I can reduce the days to 18 hours.' If you could do this you would have total control of the resource. But, of course you cannot, as the amount of time and the rate at which it is expended is a given. What you can manage is what you achieve in the time available. Again, this is about mindset. Thinking this way will mean that you are more focused and in control.

3. *My focus must be on results, then I can organise my time to spend on activities that contribute to those results*

The distinction between activity and output is paramount. We can fall into the trap of thinking that if we are busy then we are making most use of time. This is conditioning, as it feels moral to be busy, that you are 'earning your keep'. However, activity is not necessarily the same as effectiveness. A focus on results involves stepping back, resisting the inclination to roll your sleeves up and be busy.

Some time ago I was working with a team of managers in a workshop. The managing director of the business, who was visiting, asked them a question: 'How would you feel if, when I walked into your office, you were sitting there in a relaxed manner – no paper on your desk, clearly not involved in any activity?' To a person, they all replied 'guilty'. The managing director replied that he wanted them to step back and think about plans and strategy rather than always be putting out bush fires. He was trying to make the point that output was not related to frantic activity.

Of course there is also the question that, if these managers felt guilty about apparent 'non-activity', then maybe the managing director was himself sending out the wrong messages . . . But that is another story!

4. My own discipline will determine my level of effectiveness

We are all human. We tend to blame others, outside factors, as the cause of our woes. There is a tendency to blame colleagues, staff, the boss, customers, interruptions and sidetracks as the prime reasons for running out of time, for not completing the jobs that we had intended to. Of course these are factors and we will be discussing ways to manage them. However, our own lack of discipline contributes to time being lost. Effective time management is about *self-discipline*.

Let's be honest; there are times when our own lack of focus leads to time being spent ineffectively. We start a job we know is important but we do not really want to do it; we think of reasons to get involved in something else. Are you a prevaricator? Do you spend time debating what to do when the answer is obvious? During the time it has taken to reach a decision about what to do the job could have been done.

However, this is not a recipe for making you a machine! There are occasions when you want, and indeed, need the float of 'do nothing' time. This is fine, as long as you are aware of it, and the percentage of such time is kept within reasonable boundaries. The essence of this self-discipline commandment is again about the level of control that you have.

5. *While I acknowledge that some events are outside of my control, I must be prepared and able to manage their impacts on my time*

We have already established that some events are outside of your control. This is reality. Acknowledging this can help reduce stress, as you realise that you are not responsible for everything. However, it is not a licence to abdicate responsibility altogether! You still have to manage these events that are outside of your control, and manage their impacts. How you manage these events, the amount of time you spend on them, will be specific to each situation.

We will be covering how you make these decisions in subsequent chapters. For the moment we are not going to get immersed in specific actions – we are still in the step back phase, looking at the principles, the items in the mindset you require. The importance of this fifth commandment is that acknowledging that some factors are outside your control does not mean that you do not have a responsibility to manage their impacts.

6. *If I am not being effective I will impact on the effectiveness of my colleagues*

No one is an island. In Commandment 4 I stated that while your own self-discipline determines your time effectiveness, outside factors – other people – also have an impact. This is a two-way street – your actions, your time management, or lack of it, will impact on others.

This is contrary to what I believe is a popular perception that how an individual manages their time impacts on them and them only. This is just not true! How many times have you experienced the following? A manager or a colleague asks you to complete a task (provide data, produce a report, etc.) that is really urgent, something that they must have by yesterday if possible. The reason may be quite legitimate, say an unexpected demand that suddenly landed on their desk. However, I believe that in a high percentage of cases the demand did not suddenly appear, it had been on their list of things to do for some time. They had not planned ahead, so it became a crisis. That person's lack of planning and time management now impacts on your time, your schedules.

However, the question is, how many times do you do this to other people?

7. *My vision must always be of three time dimensions – short, medium and long term*

In business terms the percentage of time you spend on each of these will be largely dependent on your role. For example, a marketing director would be spending more time on long-term issues than, say, a team leader in a busy sales office. One role is more strategically focused, the other more operational. In terms of our private lives we should always be thinking across these timeframes, but again the balance will be driven by where we are in our lives.

One of the issues for busy people is that because there are always so many short-term goals and actions they can take up all of the available time. This is understandable, but it is a trap. Focusing only on the short term consigns you to a treadmill, where the danger is that you are being driven by events rather than controlling them.

Achieving the balance is the key. Having medium- and long-term visions, and planning to realise them at the same time as managing the here and now, is one of the keys to time management.

8. *The planned must coexist with the non-planned – sometimes the non-planned will take priority*

An element of time management is planning, and we will be discussing this in depth in Part 3. However, in the real world we cannot plan for everything. In fact, over-planning resulting in an overly rigid schedule with no in-built flexibility can be as damaging as no planning at all.

The rule is to plan what you can plan for, while being able to respond to the things you cannot plan for in the most effective way. We know that virtually every day we will have to manage things we did not and cannot plan for. We know they will happen. What we do not know is exactly what they will be or when during the day they will happen. Someone who is over-planned, is too rigid in their thinking, will tend to see these non-planned items as problems and interruptions. They may well be. But they may also be more significant, more important than the tasks you had planned to complete.

It is all about priorities. The effective time manager is able to balance the planned and the non-planned. The key is to *respond* to the non-planned rather than react. Reaction is 'knee jerk', with no thought. Response is considered. Later I will be providing you with some tools and guidelines to help you manage the balance between the two.

9. *I must select the tasks I spend my time on based primarily on their level of importance, not the 'urgency label' attached to them*

My experience is that this requires the biggest mindset shift of all for many people. On numerous occasions when I have said to participants attending time management workshops, 'from today you will no longer prioritise your time based on the urgency of the tasks involved, but on their importance or contribution', I have met resistance. As the concept is developed, as the workshop unfolds, generally people have accepted the principle.

The initial reaction of rejection is understandable. We are conditioned to react to 'urgent labels' and we are inundated by claims that this or that is 'urgent'. The implication is that you must drop everything and do it now! Have you noticed the Post-it message pads with the 'Urgent message' at the top? The problem is that we react as if the message really is urgent and indeed important! Now, some urgent actions may indeed be important – this is fine. Action them! It is not about ignoring urgent actions. What it is about is determining when you complete tasks, and how much time you allocate to them based *primarily* on the importance of the task (i.e. its contribution to your objectives) rather than the urgency label. While the time scale is a factor in the planning and allocation of time, it is not the prime driver.

Finally on the subject of reacting to 'urgent tags', have you ever experienced the following? You have been asked by a colleague to help them out, to produce a report for them. They need it urgently. It is a matter of life and death, the business could fold if the data is not available now. You help out, you leave what you are doing and produce the report. Two days later you see your colleague by the coffee machine.

'Was the report OK?' you ask.

'Yes, fine. I haven't had a chance to look at it in detail yet, but thanks anyway,' comes the reply.

So, beware of tasks with urgent labels!

10. *I must have conviction if I am going to hold on to and protect my priorities . . .be ruthless with time and gracious with people*

Conviction – what has this got to do with time management? Conviction is about being prepared to hold on to your plans and priorities in the face of the demands and pressures to drag you away from them. I have said that the non-planned may take priority over the planned. If so, this is legitimate, so your plans change. However, some sidetracks and interruptions to your plans will not be legitimate. They need to be fended off, to be managed. This will involve saying no to people.

Again I am not preaching anarchy! You are not giving an automatic no response, but after considering the situation, and responding to a demand on your time, you may well be saying no, *not now*. This involves managing the situation from a factual and relationship aspect. Pushing back, saying no not now, particularly to your boss, may take courage. It certainly requires conviction.

Summary

Each of these 'Ten Commandments' or principles will be developed as you proceed through the book. Each reader will of course react to them differently. You may be thinking 'I accept most of them but not all', while another reader will express a different view. I do not expect everybody to buy all of these 100% at this stage, but I urge you to keep an open mind as I genuinely believe that they are the foundations for effective time management. As with all learning it is not wise to try change everything at the same time.

Use the chart on the next two pages to assess the degree to which your current values match with those expressed in the 'Ten Commandments' of time management. Use the 1–10 scale to help you arrive at your conclusions. Score 1 for an item where you feel you totally disagree and 10 where you feel that there is total congruence. When you have completed this go through the list and indicate with an asterisk the top three – where you feel you would gain most benefit by adopting and practising that value. You can use this as one of the planning points for developing your personal time management strategy.

1. I am aware that time is a non-reuseable resource, that I cannot take the last hour back and use it more effectively

| 1 | 2 | 3 | 4 | 5 | 6 | 7 | 8 | 9 | 10 |

2. Given 1, I cannot manage time, but I can manage what I achieve within the time available

| 1 | 2 | 3 | 4 | 5 | 6 | 7 | 8 | 9 | 10 |

3. My focus must be on results, then I can organise my time to spend on activities that contribute to results

| 1 | 2 | 3 | 4 | 5 | 6 | 7 | 8 | 9 | 10 |

4. My own discipline will determine my level of effectiveness

| 1 | 2 | 3 | 4 | 5 | 6 | 7 | 8 | 9 | 10 |

5. While I acknowledge that some events are outside of my control, I must be prepared and able to manage their impacts on my time

| 1 | 2 | 3 | 4 | 5 | 6 | 7 | 8 | 9 | 10 |

6. If I am not being effective, I will impact on the effectiveness of my colleagues

| 1 | 2 | 3 | 4 | 5 | 6 | 7 | 8 | 9 | 10 |

7. My vision must always be of three time dimensions – short, medium and long term.

| 1 | 2 | 3 | 4 | 5 | 6 | 7 | 8 | 9 | 10 |

8. The planned must coexist with the non-planned – sometimes the non-planned will take priority

| 1 | 2 | 3 | 4 | 5 | 6 | 7 | 8 | 9 | 10 |

9. I must select the tasks I spend my time on based primarily on their level of importance, not the 'urgency label' attached to them

| 1 | 2 | 3 | 4 | 5 | 6 | 7 | 8 | 9 | 10 |

10. I must have conviction if I am going to hold on to and protect my priorities – be ruthless with time and gracious with people

| 1 | 2 | 3 | 4 | 5 | 6 | 7 | 8 | 9 | 10 |

CHAPTER 3

Introducing the three-point model

In the introduction and the first two chapters my aim has been to encourage you to step back and think about the subject of time, and the challenges you face when working towards what you want to achieve in both life and work terms. One of the key messages so far is that time management techniques, important as they are, on their own will not solve time management problems. This is why I have introduced the beliefs and values – the mindset items – early on. These may have stimulated your thinking and possibly encouraged you to see the subject from a different perspective. I hope so.

However, you may be thinking that this all makes common sense in theory – 'but how am I going to overcome the time management issues that I have? Please give me some practical answers!' This is exactly the intention of the book, and from Part 2 onwards I will be giving you some step by step guidelines, many of which you can implement immediately. But please retain the learning points from the initial chapters, as they provide the right context for developing your own practical time management plan. Remember that effective time management is about mindset as well as techniques.

To provide a framework for the body of the book I will introduce you to a three-point model for achieving time effectiveness. This will provide a logical structure, and make it easier for you to develop your own plans.

Before I do this let us be clear about what we mean by 'effectiveness'. It is a term that is often used, not just in relation to time management. What does it mean? There is often confusion between 'effectiveness' and 'efficiency'. They are different, and in the context of time management this difference is critical.

To be efficient is to do things well – to provide a quality, accurate output. Effectiveness has one additional word in its definition – to do the *right* things well. Let me give you an example to demonstrate the importance of the difference.

You are the manager in charge of finance for a medium-sized company; ten people work in your department. You used work in the team before you were made head of department. Every month you spend 1.5 days checking the month-end reports to ensure that they are accurate. This is a mechanical task, but it is one that you are comfortable with as you have been doing it since you were a junior clerk. Unquestionably you are efficient, in that you can do the job well. But are you being effective? As the finance manager is this good use of your time? One of the key themes that we will develop is that good time managers focus on the priorities, the tasks that are high contributors.

Helping you to achieve this focus is one of the principal aims of the three point model, illustrated in Figure 3.1 below.

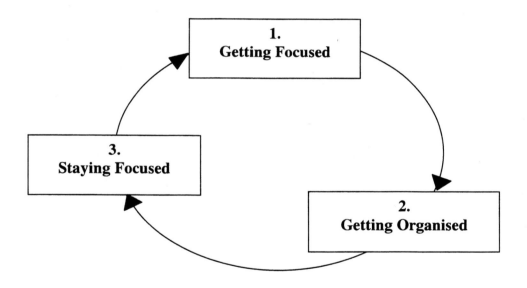

Figure 3.1 The three-point model.

1. *Getting focused.* This about being clear about goals and results. In work terms you are employed to deliver results. You have a defined job role, and usually this includes a

statement of key objectives and goals. If you run your own business you will not have this discipline 'imposed' on you, so your own discipline and focus is even more crucial. Life goals require this same discipline, as they are self-driven rather than being directed from elsewhere. As with efficiency and effectiveness there can be a confusion between results and tasks. Some people, asked what they are employed to do, will list the tasks they carry out when they should be describing their goals. Goals are different to tasks – tasks are only the means to achieve the goal. You cannot be an effective time manager without clarity, without being focused on what your goals are.

2. *Getting organised.* Once focused on the goals and result areas you need to organise yourself so that you concentrate on the tasks and activities that will be contributors to their achievement. Being organised is typically seen as the sole factor in possessing time management skills. An ability to be organised and structured is of course important, and Part 3 is devoted to this. However, organisation is only relevant if it is focused on the goals and the result areas.

3. *Staying focused.* Getting focused and getting organised are mainly to do with planning. Staying focused is about ensuring that your plans are converted into reality. I have already briefly discussed the issues of managing the sidetracks, the interruptions, the unexpected. In day-to-day

business, and at a life level, there will be numerous factors that can – and often do – divert you from your intentions. Staying focused means holding onto your plans in the face of the day-to-day realities. Also, you must remember that at times responding to the unexpected is the right thing to do, as it assumes a greater priority than the planned. There are a number of skills involved in staying focused – the skills to manage people and relationships as well as the situations themselves. Part 4 covers in detail the range of skills that need to be developed and applied.

Use the model as a guideline, to develop a way of thinking for how you manage yourself and the time available to you. It is not intended to impose a rigid structure on you! Given the dynamics and variables in our work and our lives a set of rules is not the answer. Think of it as providing a framework.

PART 1

Stepping back – key messages and action plan

- There are no magic solutions. Improving time management involves changing and developing a number of aspects of how you plan and organise your time. Collectively they will produce results.

- Create a balance in your life by paying attention to 'in work' and 'out of work time'. There is no set formula – the correct balance will be driven by your individual circumstances and priorities. Work on creating the balance that is right for you.

- It is widely recognised that the workaholic is detrimental to themselves, and in the long term is not effective for their employer.

- Some investment in time will be needed to become more effective in managing time. You will receive a payback in the mid and long term if you commit to the investment.

- Effective time management requires more than 'techniques'. Mindset – your way of thinking – is as important as technique.

- Do not see time as an enemy. View it as a valuable resource, a resource which cannot be reused.

- Generally you have more control of what you achieve in the time available than you think. Feeling in control reduces the stress caused by time pressures.

- The 'Ten Commandments' of effective time management provide the foundations for developing a positive set of principles and values to help you take control of time.

- The three-point model – getting focused, getting organised, staying focused – provides a practical framework for implementing the principles described in the Ten Commandments.

Committing intentions to writing, I believe, increases the likelihood of the intentions being put into action and converted into reality. This is why I have included a 'points for action' section at the end of each part. The questions are designed to encourage you to reflect on the key learning points, and to capture the actions that you intend to take to develop your time management skills. Use the chart on the following page to log your points. Alternatively, if you have a time system already set up include a section in it to record the actions.

Investing time now and at the end of each part will help you when completing the final activity in the book, 'where do you go from here'. This is designed to help you formulate your own time management development plan when you have completed *Taming Time*. Remember that one of the key messages is that you need to invest time to make time. So, invest ten minutes now before moving on to Part 2.

Record everything in pencil. As you progress through the book you may decide to revisit some of these priorities and change them. Finally, I have asked you to list no more than five actions. This is to force you to focus and prioritise. Over-committing to many things is not realistic and does not lead to good time management.

Part 1

Points for action

What have been the major learning points from this part of the book?
1.
2.
3.
4.
5.

What specific actions do you intend to take to develop your time management effectiveness? Select no more than *five* actions and list in priority sequence. Prioritise based on the positive impact you believe the action will have. Commit to timescales – when you intend to implement the action.
1.
2.
3.
4.
5.

PART 2

Getting focused

CHAPTER 4

Why am I here?

You cannot plan your journey until you are clear about the destination. In time management terms the destination is your goal. In reality you may have more than one goal, so a number of journeys will need to be planned. Planning the journey involves defining the actions you need to take, and allocating time to complete them, as a means of reaching your goals.

The answer to the question 'why am I here?' is *to achieve your goals*. This may sound obvious, but it is surprising how many people involve themselves in tasks and activities without having really thought through what they are seeking to achieve. It is easy to fall into the activity trap, and see tasks as an end in themselves. In fact tasks and activities are only a means to an end – to contribute to and to move you closer to reaching your goals.

I have described a goal as the destination of a journey. Goals can also be described as desired results, the output, from activity.

Goals represent achievement. You may be more comfortable using the term objective or even target. The label you use is unimportant – what is important is that there is agreement that getting focused is about being clear about what you want to achieve.

In Part 1 I introduced the theme that we should be considering time management in life terms, not just work terms. Achieving the balance between in work and out of work time is key. You will be more effective in your work if you achieve that balance. Therefore being clear about your goals in life terms is important. In a sense it is understandable that we have a greater clarity in our work goals than broader life goals. For many who are working in large corporations there are processes – for example appraisals, reviews, performance management systems – that provide the mechanism for periodically reviewing direction, goals and targets. So you are driven to consider your destination, and of course some goals will be a given, driven from above.

There is not the same external discipline to make you focus on your life goals, so that discipline must come from within. Also, most people are busy people – the time involved in reaching the work goals becomes all-consuming. Therefore there is a risk that we do not take the time to consider the broader life goals at all.

The two sets of goals are not necessarily in conflict, and the greater the degree of congruence between the two the greater the degree of harmony that you will enjoy. For example, you may have a life goal of experiencing living in a different country. The company you work for is international, and if you can progress to the next job level in your career then there are opportunities for a secondment to an overseas subsidiary. Here there is congruence and common ground.

Of course there can also be conflict – for example, you are successful in your career as an account manager for a large computer company. Your promotional prospects and income expectations are good. However, you have a passionate life goal to be involved in charity work in a third world country. Unless the company you work for has a policy of releasing people for such projects then it would seem there is a conflict between the two goals. You then must ask yourself which is more important, what is practical, what other responsibilities you have, how can you fund your life goal, etc. There are no easy decisions. You must decide your own priorities, and how you are going to realise them. The dream goal is not always possible, but by modifying your goals you may be able to satisfy your work and life aspirations.

To help you create some focus answer the four questions below. Think in terms of life and work goals.

1. What are your priority goals for the next three months?

2. What are your priority goals for the next six months?

3. What are your priority goals for the next twelve months?

4. You have six months to leave your mark. What achievement do you want to be remembered for?

You may have written the same goal for three, six and twelve months. This is fine – it may be a long-term goal that you are working to in stages. You may have a combination of life and work goals, or just work goals. This is also fine. You may have made the decision that, given where you are in your career, your focus will be on achieving work goals for the next twelve months, provided you have considered your broader life goals and made the conscious decision that for the period in question the work related goals are the legitimate priorities. This is different to not considering the broader life goals at all. You are in charge of your own priorities!

People's answers to question 4 – leaving your mark – are usually interesting. I have asked this question numerous times of participants on time management workshops. The six-month time limit, the finality, creates a focus and makes you consider what really is important. Generally the responses are life-related, not work-specific, goals.

In summary, getting focused is about being clear about what you want to achieve, what your goals are in life and work terms. In the next chapter we will discuss how you can express these goals more clearly.

CHAPTER 5

Thinking smart

'I want to get fitter,' states the business person who feels that the desk bound job does nothing for physical fitness.

'I am going to sell more,' states the ambitious sales person.

Are these people getting focused? In a sense they are in that they are expressing something they want to achieve. However, the statements are vague, and are in reality no more than broad aims, statements of intent. The problem with such broad statements is that they are not providing a measuring point for achievement, and as such provide a 'get out'.

Let us consider the two statements. Let's look first at the 'I am going to get fit' statement. How do I define fit? When is the fitness programme going to start? How is progress going to be measured? Now think about the second statement, 'I am going to sell more'. How do I define more? Over what time period and by when? What are going to be the measures of success?

Returning to the destination analogy, the above statements are describing a general direction, for example 'I am going to head north'. This statement does not define the exact location or the planned time of arrival. However, being focused means that you state your goals in precise terms. Why is this important? It is all too easy not to be committed to broad statements of intent. Let us have some honesty time! We all have things we have the intention to achieve, or aspects of our lives that we want to change, that have stayed as intentions for some time, probably for years in some cases. They are always in the backs of our minds and they come to the forefront now and again, but they stay as intentions. Things will only move forward by converting that aim into something specific, something measurable. The act of simply writing the goal down in clear concise terms will increase the percentage chance of action being taken.

Working with 'smart goals' is a well tried and established method of creating the focus that will lead to action. In fact the acronym SMART describes the characteristics of a highly focused goal statement, as you can see from Figure 5.1.

I do not expect you to spend hours designing goal statements that precisely fit the five criteria in the diagram – that would be bad use of time! Consider it as a way of thinking, so again it is a mindset item. You can use it as a checklist to ensure that in defining your goals you are creating the correct level of focus.

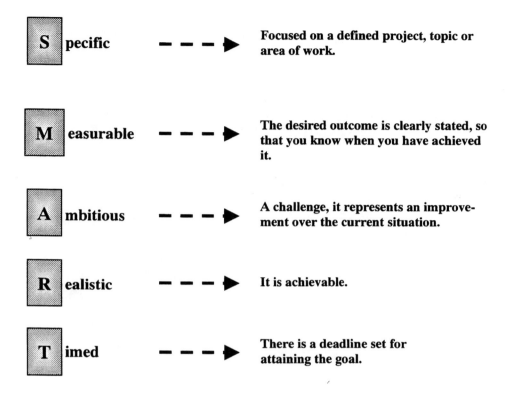

Figure 5.1 'Smart' goals.

Let's return to the aspiring athlete and the aspiring sales person.

'I want to get fitter' in 'smart' terms could read: 'My objective is to be able to complete three aerobic workouts of a minimum of one hour each, during which I complete ten kilometres in each one either running, cycling, rowing or a combination. I aim to reach this standard within six months.'

Now this may sound very formal to describe a recreational goal, and I am not suggesting that you put yourself under possible stress to do so! However, as an example it illustrates how a broad statement of aim can be converted to a very focused goal by using the 'smart' criteria.

If we return to the sales person who wants to sell more – in 'smart' terms the goal could be: 'To achieve sales of one million in turnover next year which represents an increase of 15% over this year's performance'. Again the example illustrates how, by conforming to 'smart', we can convert an intention into something that is highly specific and measurable.

In both cases, the destination, the desired result, is absolutely clear. As I have already said you cannot plan anything until you have decided on your destination. Smart goals provide the destination, from which you can start to plan the actions you must take to get there.

CHAPTER 6

The three time frames

I am sure that you are all familiar with the term 'crisis management'. Crisis managers are usually working on the principle, often unconsciously, that everything becomes urgent eventually, and that is the time to react to it! The problem with this approach is that you are locked into one time frame only – the short term, the immediate. Once locked into this you are there forever, as the reactive management, being driven as opposed to doing the driving, becomes a self-fulfilling prophesy. You are on a treadmill – unless you take action to break out of the short-term cycle.

Of course the immediate, the here and now, has to be managed. For many of us that is a key part of our job responsibilities – to manage the unexpected, the problems. The same is true in our private lives. Those of you with partners and families will be familiar with the time involved in managing relationships, the children, their issues, their concerns about school, etc.! So, the here and now is a reality. We all have to manage this and it is right that we should.

However, being locked into short-termism restricts us to tasks and actions. At the extreme, stepping back and thinking about goals becomes non-existent. Frankly, there is no time!

Therefore, in terms of 'getting focused' we need to have three time frames in our minds – short, medium and long term. Taking this approach will avoid the short-term time trap which restricts us to reacting to the here and now, and stops us taking control of the future. This will be helpful in planning your work and career goals as well as your broader life goals. Some plans will represent long-term goals, but you can define short- and medium-term goals which are stepping stones to the longer term. Think of the destination analogy again. Say you are planning to drive to Spain. In this simplistic example, the long-term, say, three-day goal is to reach Madrid. Your short-term goal, starting from the centre of the UK, is to reach Paris by the end of day one; your medium-term goal is to reach the French–Spanish border by the end of day two. The short-term goals, often called intermediate goals or milestones, will simplify planning the actions to attain the long-term goal. You are breaking it down into more manageable bites. Some short-term goals are end goals in their own right.

In work and life terms three days can hardly be defined as long term! So how do we define these three time frames? There are no hard and fast rules. In work terms the time frames will be driven by the job role. For example, a chief executive may define short term as one year, medium term as two years and long term as five years. This is because in such a role the focus will tend to be on the longer-term strategic issues and plans. Someone who is managing a busy, event-driven accounts office will most probably have different frames of reference. For them short term may be defined as a month, medium term three months and long term one year. The important thing is that you develop your own way of working to be setting goals across the three time frames. Decide what you think is appropriate for you. Nothing need be fixed forever – you can refine the time frames any time you wish. As a general guide, for work goals think in terms of the time frames shown in Figure 6.1.

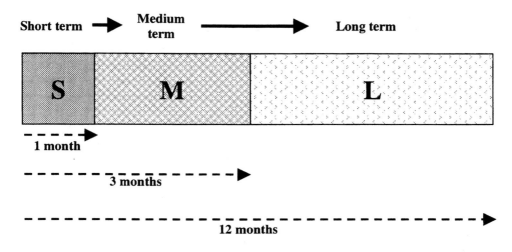

Figure 6.1 The three time frames.

In considering life goals you may want to define different time scales. For example, a long-term life goal may be five years. Again, no rules – you decide what is appropriate for you.

In summary, avoid the trap of short-termism by have three time frames for your goals – short, medium and long term.

PART 2

Getting focused – key messages and action plan

- You cannot plan your journey until you are clear about the destination.

- Your goals represent the destination. Goals, or objectives, describe what you want to achieve, the outputs from your activities.

- Job and life goals can be complimentary. If there is a conflict you will need to prioritise and assess the reality of achieving both.

- Think 'smart'. Define you goals in 'smart' terms.

- 'Smart' is an acronym for specific, measurable, ambitious, realistic and timed.

- Use these smart characteristics when defining your goals to ensure that you are clear and concise in what you want to achieve.

- Think across three time frames when setting your goals – short, medium and long term.

You can simplify planning your long-term goals by defining short- and medium-term goals that represent milestones in attaining the long term.

Part 2

Points for action

What have been the major learning points from this part of the book?
1.
2.
3.
4.
5.

What specific actions do you intend to take to develop your time management effectiveness? Select no more than *five* actions and list in priority sequence. Prioritise based on the positive impact you believe the action will have. Commit to timescales – when you intend to implement the action.
1.
2.
3.
4.
5.

PART 3

Getting organised

CHAPTER 7

Putting order into chaos

You are now focused. You are clear about your work and life goals; they are described in smart terms; you have short-, medium- and long-term goals. The second element in the three-point model is getting organised. This is about organising ourselves so that we concentrate on the action, tasks and projects that will contribute to the achievement of those goals. Activity, the right type of activity, is the means to achieving results. Returning to the destination analogy, getting organised involves planning the trip, setting off on the journey, and completing the actions you need to take arrive on schedule.

Of course we are all aware that being focused on a goal and achieving it are two different things! A lot of work and energy is involved in transforming the intention into a reality. One of the issues we have to face is that most of us most of the time have a heavy workload, lists of actions to complete, all seemingly with yesterday's deadlines. This can mean chaos.

How often does your working day feel like chaos? The items to action list gets longer rather than shorter, the number of interruptions keep taking you away from the things you had intended to do, you feel the stress building up, the dream of leaving on time fades. You have the distinct feeling that you are not controlling events, they are controlling you. You are glad to have survived at least! You ask the questions, what have I achieved? what contribution to my goals have I made? The work chaos then spins into your out of work life. You arrive home late, maybe with some work to do. This impacts on your ability to focus on your recreational and life goals.

In the above, possibly I am describing an extreme case. However, research suggests that what I have described is the reality for a number of us. The way forward – and I repeat a point that I have made before that to which there are no magic answers – is to put some order into the chaos. This is the essence of this part of the book – to provide you with some guidelines, to enable you to take control. At the same time we must acknowledge that we do not live in a perfect world, and that we cannot control everything. Acknowledging that there will always be a level of chaos is important, and in Chapter 9 we look at how you can even thrive on it.

The first step in getting organised, and to putting order into chaos, is to understand the different types of tasks and activities you are involved in. Categorisation of tasks will give you some clarity as to how much time you should be allocating to each, in the context of the contribution they make to the achievement of your goals. This clarity and understanding can form the basis for your time planning.

Before we look at the different task categories let me highlight a fundamental point – that not everything can be planned. Therefore you should not try to plan everything. However, you should plan everything that can be planned.

There are three categories of tasks that you have to address. I strongly believe that these categories, which are explained further below, are valid and helpful for any job role. You can also apply them to your out of work time and plans.

Managing 'now' tasks

These are tasks that you *can* plan. You can think of these as maintenance tasks. In most jobs there are a number of things that need to be completed to ensure the smooth running of a business or department, or to meet the standards required. Completion of these tasks ensures that the 'engine' of the business performs so that the current objectives are achieved. They may be seen as routine tasks, but this does not mean that they are unimportant.

What makes up your management of 'now' tasks will obviously be driven by your job and role. Examples may be as follows:

- attendance at weekly departmental meetings;
- completion of monthly reports;
- responding to customer enquiries;
- ordering supplies;
- processing customer orders;
- system maintenance;
- financial reporting.

Given that these are known tasks, they can be planned, and should form the basis of your time planning. As they are known tasks, allocating time to them accurately should be straightforward. It can also be helpful to label these tasks as daily, weekly or monthly. How much of your working week is devoted to these tasks will again be role-specific. For example, a supervisor in a call centre is more likely to allocate a greater percentage of their total time to such tasks than a marketing director who would be more focused on the future.

Forming 'future' tasks

These are the tasks that contribute to positive change. These are also tasks that you can plan. They represent the actions you need to take to achieve the short-, medium- and long-term goals that you have defined or have been set for you. These are developmental activities.

Therefore allocating time to these tasks is crucial. These are the tasks that will bring about improvements and success, the tasks that will make a difference. They guarantee the long term. As with the management of 'now' tasks, these 'future' tasks will be driven by your job role. Examples may be:

- a self-development programme;
- coaching team members;
- developing new procedures so that effectiveness can be improved;
- involvement in projects relating to organisation, business or systems development;
- meeting with customers to discuss new projects and contracts;
- working on product and service development;
- continuous improvement initiatives.

The percentage of your time allocated to this category of task will again be driven by your role. For example, a managing director should be spending the majority of his or her time on forming the future. On the other hand, someone supervising a maintenance team in a production environment is more likely to spend their time on more immediate actions.

Non-planned tasks

As the heading suggests these tasks cannot be planned! I think that without exception everybody, regardless of the job role, has to manage the unplanned. Without the unplanned time management would be a lot simpler as it is often the unexpected that causes the chaos and the feeling of not being in control. The first step is to accept the non-planned as a reality. They go with the territory, they are part of the job. The second step is to have a time plan that has sufficient flex to respond to the unexpected. The previous task categories can be planned and should form the basis of your daily, weekly and monthly plans, while ensuring that you allocate time for the unexpected events. You know that these will happen. What you do not know is when, their exact nature, and how long they will take to resolve.

Examples of non-planned tasks, again dependent on your job role, may be:

- an urgent customer request;
- the computer system goes down;
- supplies that you urgently need are delayed;
- a demand from the boss!

- a member of your team being ill – you have a resource problem;

- a change of priority.

Finally, in considering the unplanned there are two important points to remember. Firstly, the unexpected may take priority over the planned. Secondly, a percentage of the unplanned may be avoidable in the future. If you analyse the nature of the non-planned you may find that while each incident may be unique in detail, there is a common cause. The non-planned involve us in reaction, overcoming the immediate problem. By stepping back and thinking about the root cause, you may be able to take proactive action to prevent or minimise their occurrence in the future. So over time there may be the possibility to reduce the percentage of your time reacting to the unexpected.

Putting order into chaos

How can categorising tasks into these three categories help you put order into chaos and get organised?

- Define the 'now' tasks that are relevant for you and make these the basis for designing your time plans. They are a given, and you can size these tasks in terms of how long they will take so there is a high level of predictability. Further define them into daily, weekly or monthly tasks and allocate time accordingly.

- Define the 'future' tasks that are relevant to you. These tasks can also be planned, and time allocated to them. These activities become the second stage in the construction of your time plan. In considering these remember that by their very nature they will often relate to long-term goals. This gives you the opportunity to allocate time into the future, hence giving you the basis for medium- and long-term activity planning.

- It is important that you achieve the correct balance between the 'now' and 'future' tasks. If all you are doing is completing the 'now' tasks then there will be no future development, no future improvements – 'if all you do is maintain you stay where you are'. However, managing now is also important. If you cannot manage today there is no tomorrow!

- Avoid over-planning your time with the planned tasks. You know that the unexpected will happen, so you must cater for it. Take time to analyse the non-planned, in terms of when they occur and how much of your working day is taken up with them. Of course predicting the future in this way cannot be precise, but you will build a view as to how much non-committed time you need to allocate.

- The unexpected may take priority over the planned so do not see the non-planned as automatically invalid interruptions.

We will cover how to prioritise and make the right decisions in the next chapter.

- Take some time to analyse the nature and the reasons for the unexpected. There may be actions you can take to minimise it in the future. Make this analysis one of your planned forming the future tasks!

Conclusion

Before you move on to the next chapter take some time to complete the following:

- Make a list of your planned 'now' tasks. List them as daily, weekly or monthly activities.

- List the actions relating to your 'future' tasks, those that will contribute to the achievement of the medium- and long-term goals. You may find it useful to list them under different project categories.

- Brainstorm a list, based on your last 30 days' experience, of the significant non-planned tasks.

You will be able to use this information to start time planning when we move on to discuss prioritising and using a system.

CHAPTER 8

Prioritising

What is prioritisation?

In my experience the ability to prioritise is one of the most important time management skills. There are two reasons for this.

- Prioritising will help you to define when you decide to action tasks and how much time to allocate to them. This is crucial if you are going to effectively manage the level and range of tasks – the 'now', the 'future', the unplanned – that demand your attention.

- There will be times when, quite simply, there are too many things to do and not enough time. Some of you may feel that this is your norm! In this case being able to prioritise will be very important to you. In a 'not enough' time situation panic can set in – the temptation is to try and tackle all of the outstanding tasks (often in random order) in double quick time in an attempt to beat the clock. The simple answer is that if there is not enough time then you cannot complete everything unless you overestimated how much time was needed in the first place. Given the rule in life that most things take longer than you planned this is unlikely! There is only one answer – some things will not get done, or more specifically they will not get done now. You have to make decisions about what gets done now and what must be rescheduled – this is prioritising. Prioritising is not about deciding not to do things but about deciding when you do them.

In Chapter 2 I introduced you to the 'Ten Commandments' of time management. Commandment 9 is 'I must select my tasks I spend my time on based primarily on their level of importance, not the "urgency label" attached to them'. I also stated that for many this requires the biggest shift in mindset as we are conditioned to react to the urgent label. In this context I am defining importance as the level of contribution to the achievement of goals. You will recall in Chapter 4, 'Why am I here?' I covered the point that your purpose is to achieve results and outcomes, in other words reach your goals. Tasks and actions are a means to that end. Therefore it is logical that you allocate time to the high contribution tasks and in the 'not enough time situations' you prioritise based on importance.

I must stress that this does not mean that you ignore timescales and urgency. That is unrealistic, as in our lives both in and out of work we are bound by certain deadlines. What it does mean is that in carrying out a prioritising exercise you have to go through a two-stage process. Now you may be thinking that a two-stage process is going to take time. Correct! However, it will not take as much time as you may imagine, and you also need to remember the rule that you will have to invest time to make time. Investing time in prioritising will give you a payback (of time) on that investment.

So how do you prioritise? Let me take what is probably a typical situation. You are having one of 'those' days. It is now mid-afternoon. There are a number of tasks you had planned to action today, but you have only managed to complete half of them. In addition a number of unplanned actions have landed on your desk. Staying late at work is not an option as you have family commitments this evening. You are staring at the list of actions. Where do you start? Having a method of prioritising will enable you to put order into the chaos.

A practical system of prioritisation

There are a number of prioritisation models available. I recommend a practical system that you can use on a daily basis with the minimum investment of time. It works as follows.

First, rank the tasks you have to complete on their levels of importance. To restate, we are defining importance as level of contribution to the achievement of your goals – in other words the impact of the task on achievement. Rank each task as having high, medium or low importance/impact. You can set up your own coding system but I suggest you use an A, B or C categorisation. Tasks coded A are high importance, B tasks medium importance, C tasks low importance. The benefit of using this labelling is that it is widely used – for example, Time/system, one of the leading suppliers of time management systems, employ this method. So, if you decided to use a Time/system product you would be using common language.

Second, categorise on urgency. Urgency is the about timescale, when the task must be completed. Remember to question the urgency labels associated with tasks. As I have already suggested people can get into the habit of saying 'this is urgent, it must be done now' without really thinking through when the task actually needs to be completed. Some actions are urgent so you cannot automatically treat an urgent request as bogus. As with coding importance you can devise your own coding system, but I would recommend you use a simple 1, 2, 3 system: code 1 items are urgent, must do now; code 2 items are 'do soon', but need not be actioned immediately; code 3 items can wait, and can be scheduled as a medium- or even long-term activity.

To summarise the system that I am suggesting:

Importance

A = High importance/impact

B = Medium importance/impact

C = Low importance/impact

Urgency

1 = Urgent, must do now

2 = Must do soon, although not required immediately

3 = Can wait, a medium- or even a long-term action

By using this coding system each task on your list is assigned an alpha-numeric code. As with other principles I have introduced you to I am not trying to impose a rigid system which forces you to code every action every day, although many people find the discipline of writing the priorities against a list very helpful. As a minimum, introduce this coding as one of your working principles, asking yourself 'which are the A, which are the B, which are the C tasks?' followed by 'what are the 1, what are the 2, what are the 3 tasks?' You should always work in that sequence – define the importance before the urgency. Again, it is a 'mindset' thing.

Using a prioritisation system cannot give you more time but it can help you be clear about what you need to do, where you need to focus your time, and what must be scheduled for action at a later date.

Let us go back to the example of mid-afternoon with too many things to do and staying late not being an option due to family commitments. The following may be the task list facing you on such an afternoon:

1. Complete monthly report for manager.

2. Produce agenda for next week's project meeting.

3. Provide information to accounts so they can resolve a customer query.

4. Respond to information request from important customer.

5. Phone your mother – she has not been very well.

6. Spend time with a colleague who has requested a 30-minute meeting.

7. Respond to three e-mails from colleagues in another location.

8. Phone an important customer to arrange a meeting that you had to postpone.

9. Organise hotels for overseas visitors who are arriving next week.

10. Book a hotel for this weekend – it is your partner's birthday treat.

11. Sit down with a team member who is having problems with certain aspects of the job.

Such a list can be daunting – where do you start? Do you simply work through from 1 to 11, even though you know that there is no way that you can complete everything? Or you can invest some time. Take five minutes, over a coffee, to review the list and identify what is important, coding each action on the A–C basis and then ranking the urgency 1–3.

Look at the list below. It is the same list as above, but the prioritisation process has taken place as shown in the right-hand column. It is only an example, so do not start debating if my prioritisation is correct or not – that would be bad use of time!

1.	Complete monthly report for manager.	A2
2.	Produce agenda for next week's project meeting.	A2
3.	Provide information to accounts so thay can resolve a customer query.	A1
4.	Respond to information request from important customer.	A1
5.	Phone your mother – she has not been very well.	A1
6.	Spend time with a colleague who has requested a 30-minute meeting.	B2
7.	Respond to three e-mails from colleagues in another location.	A2
8.	Phone an important customer to arrange a meeting that you had to postpone.	A1

9.	Organise hotels for overseas visitors who are arriving next week.	B2
10.	Book a hotel for this weekend – it is your partner's birthday treat.	A1
11.	Sit down with a team member who is having problems with certain aspects of the job.	A2

Accepting that this is only an example, what does this new picture with the relative priorities tell you? How does it help? Does it put some order into the chaos? The main change from the first list is that there are now five actions that have an A1 label – items 3, 4, 5, 8 and 10. This immediately gives you focus. These are the items to complete today. Out of these items 5, 8 and 10 are phone calls that should not take too much time. Items 3 and 4 will take the majority of the time. You can now map out the rest of the day, possibly deciding to make the phone calls first leaving you to concentrate on the two customer-related actions. You must also remember to reschedule the items you have not completed today for later in the week.

If you are cynical you may be thinking that this is all fine, but what if I had 11 A1 items on my list? This can happen, in which case you may have to negotiate with the parties involved on deadlines for some of the actions. I will be covering negotiation and other behavioural skills of time management in Part 4.

However, whatever the results of your prioritisation exercise, it is a valuable 'first pass' in helping you to schedule work effectively.

Applying the prioritisation system

The following guidelines will help you to apply this prioritisation system, and relate it to the other principles of time management.

- In theory, why should any tasks that can be planned ever get to a category 1 – urgent status? If you are thinking and planning medium and long term as well as short term, then the actions that you can plan, both the 'managing now' and 'forming the future' actions, can be scheduled and completed before they become urgent. In the real world, however, where you are dependent on other people for completion of your tasks, where priorities do change, this will not always be the case. Nevertheless, I firmly believe that most of us have a high degree of control over the tasks that can be planned if we are proactive in planning medium and long term.

    Let me give you an example. In my work as a training consultant I often meet with human resource and training managers in organisations. Without exception they find that getting line managers to provide the outputs from performance management or appraisal systems by the requested time is an ongoing problem. In most businesses the process involves periodic and annual staff reviews. The line manager with, for example, 11 direct reports to review will say that trying to complete the reviews by the required time is difficult as to conduct them will take at least a week and of course there are all of the other things to do. The argument is valid, assuming that all of the reviews need to be done in a week! But this is a long-term action that can be planned. The review process, the timescales involved, are a given. If the reviews were scheduled over, say, one month then they can be completed without them ever getting to the urgent status. So, why the panic? Because of an over-reliance on short-term planning and not enough focus on the medium and long term. Planning long term will reduce the number of code 1 urgent actions. The opposite philosophy is, as I have said before 'everything becomes urgent eventually'. Follow that path and you will always face the stress of too many urgent actions on your list of things to do.

- When planning build in some buffer time. One of the mistakes made even by some long-term planners is not building in buffer time. What do I mean by this? Assume that you have to complete a task – let's take the production of a report as an example – by the 25th of next month. You are a diligent planner, looking ahead to the medium-term tasks, so allocate the morning of the 25th to produce the report. You are planned and organised. However, what happens if, on the morning of the 25th, you are confronted by a time-consuming crisis that demands your attention? The report does not get done. You cannot deliver on the agreed date and you now have to negotiate a revised date with the person who requires the report. You are facing the stress of an urgent action that is overdue, and you may well have impacted on the plans of the person who was due to receive the report.

Is there a solution? Yes – build in a buffer. If the report was due to be completed on the 25th allocate time to do the work on the 20th. If the 20th is one of those days where, due to the unexpected, you are unable to complete the report, you still have some days available to reschedule and complete the work on time. The risk of course is that you know you have the buffer, so will let the timescales slip anyway. This is about discipline! Get into the habit of completing tasks by the buffer date and only use the safety factor in genuine emergencies. If you introduce this as part of your working practice when scheduling all planned tasks there will be a cumulative effect – you will experience less missed deadlines. Consequently you will notice that you are rescheduling tasks less, negotiating extended deadlines less. The result? You will save time.

- The prioritisation system is valuable in helping you to manage the unplanned. There are two types of poor time manager. Firstly the person who has rigid plans, a day fully scheduled with things to do, and who sees the non-planned as interruptions which should be ignored in the interests of protecting the plan. This is an interesting point; this person is a good time planner but a poor time manager, as managing includes handling the unplanned. The second type of poor time manager is the person who reacts to all of the non-planned, attempting to manage everything as it hits the desk and consequently achieving very little. A poor time planner and manager. The good time manager manages the planned *and* the non-planned. Prioritising is the key – the ability to replan and reschedule in the light of the unexpected. Let me refer back to the ten time management commandments – Commandment 8 states: 'The planned must coexist with the non planned – sometimes the non-planned will take priority'.

This says that throughout the day you will need to be revising your priorities – listing the non-planned tasks that you are receiving, deciding their priority using the A, B, C / 1, 2, 3 formula, assessing their importance and urgency against the planned actions and rescheduling as necessary. This is a key learning point: planning and prioritising are dynamic exercises which you will need to revisit frequently. The number of times you need to sit down and reassess the priorities will be driven by the level of the unplanned.

Summary

- Prioritising is one of the key time management skills.

- Keep focused on objectives. Prioritise tasks on their level of importance and contribution to objectives. Urgency, the timescale for completion, is the second level of prioritising.

- Use the A, B, C (importance) and 1, 2, 3 (urgency) codes to assess the priorities for the tasks and actions you have to complete. Alternatively, you can devise your own system.

- Use the system to assess the unplanned tasks and, accepting that some unplanned tasks will take priority over the planned, reschedule as necessary.

CHAPTER 9

Systems and discipline

One of the themes I have highlighted is that effective time management is about more than having a system. I have emphasised the importance of the 'mindset items'. However, to redress the balance, having and using a system is important – without one you cannot be an effective time manager. Effective time management is achieved via a combination of applying the principles outlined in the Ten Commandments of time management and using a system that will help you to be organised and stay organised.

Consider the number of deadlines, commitments, tasks, unexpected demands and routine actions you have to remember in, for example, the course of a month. You are probably now thinking about all of these in a work context. Now think on a broader level: add in the out of work goals and actions you are committed to. The answer you will arrive at will, I am sure, be far too many for anybody to hold in their head. Hence the need for a system.

People have challenged me on this during the early stages of time management workshops, people who reject the need for a system, saying, for example, 'I never need to write anything down, I can remember everything I need to.' Now I accept that there may be some people who have super memories and powers of recall, but I seriously doubt that we mere mortals have such capabilities! Interestingly, as the discussion continues, invariably these people will acknowledge that, yes, some things do get forgotten and that some actions do slip through the net. The other important question is how much brain power and energy is consumed trying to remember everything. I would imagine vast amounts – and unnecessarily. Having a system which enables you to log actions releases the brain and memory for more productive things. Also, by logging a task in a system means that it *can* be forgotten until the appropriate time when action is required. This has to be less stressful than having to hold everything in your head.

The other challenge I have encountered is 'I do not need a system, I write everything down on Post it notes.' We all know people like this. Their workstations are a sea of yellow! My response to such a comment is: 'Well you have a system, you are writing things down, you are logging actions – but is it an effective system?' The answer is, of course not, as the random pieces of paper are constantly being shuffled and resorted. In short merely writing things down, although writing things down is important, does not constitute a time system. Incidentally, to avoid upsetting the people who produce Post it pads, I would like to go on record as saying that I believe that they are a useful invention, and I use them frequently. However, I do not believe they were ever designed as time systems!

I acknowledge that the two examples I have given above represent an extreme and non-representative view, but they do illustrate a point that people tend to get nervous when we start talking about a system. A system implies something that controls, that is rigid. There can be the feeling that a system is fine in theory but it will not work for me.

So, what do I mean by system? In the context of time management a system is something that enables you to:

- record your short-, medium- and long-term goals;
- schedule the tasks that you need to complete to attain your goals;
- capture the non planned tasks, and schedule them for completion at the appropriate time;
- track all of your tasks and actions through to completion;
- readjust your priorities and plans as required.

At its simplest a desk diary can do much of this, as a fundamental of effective time management is good diary management.

However, most people will require more than a diary to manage the range and complexity of tasks that they need to control and put into action. This does not imply that a time system should be cumbersome and complex. An effective time system should conform to the following criteria:

1. *Take the minimum of time to administer* – to update, amend and maintain. This is one of the main fears that people have. They look at a time system – we will be appraising the range of time systems available later in this chapter – and the initial reaction is that it is complex and will take an inordinate amount of time to administer.

2. *Be flexible* – in the sense that you can personalise it to meet your own requirements. This is important as, in detail, no two job roles are the same. While we all have the same requirement to plan, capture, log, schedule and track tasks, what you need to track, and how, will be specific.

3. *Be integrated* – so that you can record, manage, schedule and track all dimensions of your goals, tasks and activities. Let me give you an example. A desk diary is sufficient to record your schedule of appointments and planned actions. But it probably lacks the flexibility and the space to capture and schedule the non-planned actions, nor is it likely to have sections dedicated to specific projects or for you to log ideas for future development, to record your goals over the three

time frames, etc. The benefit of an integrated system is that everything is in one place.

4. *Be portable* – many people spend a lot of time away from the office base. A time system needs to be with you at all times. This sounds and is an obvious point. But, for example, a time system based on a desktop PC would be inappropriate for a frequent traveller unless there is the facility to download to a laptop or other portable device.

Electronic or paper based?

There is no shortage of choice of time systems available on the market. The decision whether to select a paper-based or electronic system is purely one of personal choice, which one works best for you. My feeling is that at the top level this comes down to whether you are more comfortable with paper and pencil or keyboard and screen.

Either will meet the essential requirements of what is needed in a time system. An electronic system uses the technology to provide features that a paper-based system cannot, for example updating of your desktop system with meetings notes, changed schedules, project updates, etc. from your electronic personal organiser or palm top. This obviously saves a lot of transcription time. Against this, in my experience of watching people in meetings scheduling future meetings and agreeing future plans and actions, the person with a paper-based time system seems to get there quicker!

However, it is not my intention to mandate a specific system. I use a paper-based system as I am more comfortable with it. The features it provides meets my requirements, given my job role. However, the key is to have a system that suits you. If you use a system already, and it works for you, then stay with it. My observations if you do not currently use a time system but are now motivated to do so are as follows:

- If you are a competent PC user consider moving straight to an electronic system. There are a number of personal organisers on the market ranging from those offering basic diary and scheduling facilities to those with Internet access, e-mail facilities and connectivity with your PC. However, it is worth noting that in my experience a number of people who have migrated to an electronic system move back to a paper-based one.

- If you are not PC 'literate' then I suggest that you implement a paper-based system. Logically, you will get your time system up and running more quickly if you are not having to go through the dual learning process of coming to terms with the technology at the same time! Some people, even though they use a PC for many applications, may prefer to work with a paper time management system.

My recommendation? From what I have said already I prefer a paper-based system. I believe they provide more flexibility than electronic-based systems. I have used a Time/system Business System for a number of years. So, in a sense I have a natural bias as I am comfortable with it. It works for me and for the many, many people I have trained in time management. You can find out more about the business system, and about 'TaskTimer', their software-based product, by visiting their website at www.timesystem.co.uk. However, it's your choices. Talk with work colleagues to find out what they use and their experiences.

Features and facilities a time system needs to have

Table 9.1 lists the features and facilities a time system must have if it is going to provide you with an integrated solution. These suggestions apply equally to paper-based and electronic systems. You may want to add to the list – this is fine, as I am not trying to present you with a rigid system but with a set of guidelines which you can develop and adapt. All of the major systems will provide these features. Use this list and your additions to check out how the different systems provide these facilities and how they suit you. In my experience and in the experience of participants on time management workshops, over the first two months of using a time system you will adapt and change it until you find it meets your requirements. It should be a flexible tool which suits you, not a rigid system that dictates to you.

Table 9.1 Features/facilities of a system – minimum requirements

Year overview	To enable you to record the long-term commitments and to provide a visual of where your workload peaks may occur.
Goal setting	A section where you can record your short-, medium- and long-term goals.
Month plans	To record your medium- and long-term actions.
Daily diary	For recording your meetings, telephone contacts and planned actions.
Scratch pad	For capturing the unplanned actions so that you can then allocate time for completion in your day diary, or month plans if they are for longer-term completion.
Project plans	For logging key actions and notes relating to specific projects that you are working on.
Meeting notes	For noting the key points from meetings that you are attending and actions for you to take, to be subsequently logged in the daily diary system or forward month notes.
Telephone/address contact information	Business, private and mobile telephone numbers and e-mail and postal address information.

While I have said that this is a minimum requirement, depending on your specific job role you may decide that some of these are not required. For example, if you are a project manager you are probably working with dedicated project management systems, in which case having a project management section in your time system may well be superfluous. The key point here is not to invent applications for a time system – use it where it adds value. I repeat, it is a flexible tool, not a rigid system.

Before moving on to the next section take a few minutes to brainstorm in the grid below what additional features and facilities you feel you would need in your own time system:

1.
2.
3.
4.
5.

You have a time system, now you have to use it

Setting up a time system is a good start, but it is only a start. It requires *discipline* to maintain and update it. We are back to a mindset item again – working with your time system, updating it so that it reflects the dynamics and changes to your priorities and workload must become part of your way of working. I stress the point that having a time system, on its own, will not make you a good time manager – you have to work at it.

I am convinced that many people use a time system merely as a diary. This in itself provides a benefit, but only a fraction of the benefit compared to developing it so that it is used as an integrated planning and action tool. Time systems, paper-based or electronic, have the in-built flexibility to allow you to tailor the applications to fit your specific job requirements. Getting to the point where you have a system that works for you is the first test of discipline. I have made the point previously that I believe it will take you up to two months to arrive at a customised system that is right for you. Over these two months you will find out what parts are particularly useful and which parts you get little value from. You will also realise that you have additional requirements which you did not think of when you set the system up. This fine-tuning will take discipline and time. We return again to the principle that to make time you need to invest time. Be prepared to make that investment in the first couple of months and you will see a return.

To achieve effective use of the time system will involve an ongoing investment of your time. If working with a time system is new for you this will initially require some discipline until it has been established as a way of working – until it is, in a sense, automatic. You will need to allocate this investment time, and initially log this as a future action in your time system. Once you have logged the action you can forget about it until the appropriate time when your system will remind you.

In Table 9.2 I have defined what I believe is the average time investment on a daily, weekly, monthly and quarterly basis, and described what is involved. Use this as a guide. Add to the list as appropriate so that you arrive at your own set of time management maintenance actions.

I have not included here the time you should invest throughout the day. As we have discussed at length, your planned day will not always be the reality. There will interruptions, distractions and new priorities. So, during the day, particularly when you feel that things are spinning out of control, take a few minutes out to reprioritise and reschedule tasks as required. Resist the temptation to plough on – step back and invest a few moments to regain control.

In summary I am proposing that you invest a minimum of just over an hour per week in time planning and reviewing. Initially you may view this as extra time, but in context, given a 40-hour working week – and I am sure that many of you work longer than this – it represents approximately 2.5% of your total working time. The question you must answer is, am I going to get a good return on that investment in terms of time saved? I am confident that you will.

Table 9.2 Time investment chart.

Daily *10 mins*	Each day review the day and plan tomorrow. This involves summarising what planned actions have been completed, and what planned and unplanned actions were not completed and therefore need to be scheduled for completion tomorrow or some other point in the future. It also involves reviewing tomorrow and finalising the priorities. You can invest the 10 minutes at the end of the day or first thing the next morning.
Weekly *15 mins*	At the end of each week there are two key tasks. First, review the week just gone to ensure that all actions have been completed, or if they have not been completed have been allocated for action in the future. It is also good to ask yourself the question 'what goals have I achieved or progressed this week?' The second task is to map out the next week so that the daily plans are in place.
Monthly *20 mins*	At the end of each month review your goals, fine-tuning as necessary and looking ahead for the next 30 days to clarify the priorities, identify any potential issues (in terms of potential overload) and plan accordingly.
Quarterly *20 mins*	The purpose of the review at the end of each quarter is less about tasks and actions, but about stepping back and reviewing the medium- and long-term goals, and redefining them as necessary.

I do not want to leave you with the impression that you must become a compulsive list-maker! Without a doubt, logging your goals and actions and keeping them updated will increase the chance of action being taken, and once logged you can forget about it until you have to take that action. Writing things down will make you more effective However, a key reason for the daily, weekly, monthly and quarterly reviews is that they provide you with 'step back' time. All too often, when involved in the frantic activity of the day and the week, it is easy to lose sight of the goals and the priorities. These review times will help you regain perspective, to appraise where you are and what you are doing so that you can make a comparison with where you want to be, and thereby locate where you should be focusing your time.

Summary

- While effective time management requires more than simply using a system, you cannot be an effective time manager without one.

- If you do not use a time system already, there are a number of paper-based or electronic-based systems available.

- You must have the discipline to maintain and update your system on a regular basis. The investment required is just over one hour per week.

CHAPTER 10

Why plan if it will all change anyway?

We have now nearly finished the part of the book, which focuses on getting organised. Before we do leave this area I would like to raise a question that you may already be asking yourself. Why plan if it will all change anyway?

I can understand the feeling. Many people I have worked with on time management seminars have expressed this concern. For many, particularly those involved in very reactive, event-driven job roles or who have hectic out of work commitments, there is a feeling that no matter how much planning takes place reality will always take over. Reality is, in this sense, the crisis, the non-planned, the interruptions, the sidetracks and the diversions. Why plan? You can be fully occupied all day reacting to these events as they occur!

I understand, but I do not agree. They are excuses not reasons. Planning and organisation are two essential requirements if you are going to take control and tame time. Let me give you some compelling, and maybe at times seemingly perverse, reasons for my case.

Firstly, even if you have not completed one of the tasks you had planned, it was valid that you planned and logged it, if only for the reason that you know you did not complete it. This is the perverse argument! Let me explain. You had planned to spend time on these planned tasks for a valid reason, because they contribute to the achievement of your objectives. The benefit of having planned and logged the action, even though you failed to complete it, is you have it captured. You know that you must update your time system and reschedule it for action. Consider the alternative: not planning anything and trying to fit the tasks in if you have time The result of this will be crisis management. If the task was valid to start with, eventually you will have to devote time to it, by which time it will have a very urgent label attached to it. We come back to the key rule that you have to invest time to make time. Devoting the ten minutes a day to planning your time, even if those plans are not realised, will still be worthwhile, as you will retain control.

The second argument is also slightly perverse, but still valid. It is that if you live in a very orderly disciplined world the need for planning and organisation is reduced. Imagine you live a life and have a job where everything is totally predictable. Your job is so structured that you can define in advance exactly what will be doing on each day. Each day is the same. Each week is the same. You never encounter the unexpected, crises never happen. In such an environment, after a period of time, my guess is that you would not need to use a time system, as the predictability is such that you would remember what you would need to do. Of course I am describing a theoretical world, giving a non-realistic example. How many of us live in a world remotely like this? Most of us are having to 'multitask', to balance the planned and the unexpected, and reprioritise where we spend our time, possibly many times during a day. So, we arrive at the conclusion that the more dynamic and chaotic our environment, the greater the degree of uncertainty, the greater the need to plan and be organised. The alternative is that we are not in control – events are driving us.

As a final thought, if our lives were as predictable as in my example, we would be leading a dull and very boring existence. We need a degree of the unplanned and the unexpected!

PART 3

Getting organised – key messages and action plan

- Think of your workload as being in three task categories – 'now' tasks, 'future' tasks and non-planned tasks.

- Using these categories will help you to plan and allocate time appropriately. If you spend too much time on managing today, you will not move forward.

- The unplanned tasks may be more valid and have a greater priority than your planned tasks.

- Being able to prioritise is a key time management skill. Prioritise on importance first. This does not mean that you ignore timescales, but urgency is the second dimension after importance or contribution.

- Use an A, B, C code to allocate importance rankings. Rank urgency on a 1, 2, 3 scale. This will help you put order into the chaos and highlight where you should be spending your time.

- Careful planning of the medium and long term will reduce the number of urgent actions on your task list. In theory, there is no reason why a plannable action should ever get to the urgent category.

- Build in some buffer time, so that you have some leeway if things go wrong.

- If you do not use one already start using a time system. There are a number of paper-based and electronic systems available.

- Having a system is a starting point but you must have discipline to keep it current. Invest ten minutes a day in maintaining your time system – you will see a payback very quickly. Review your plans at the end of each week, month and quarter. Apart from helping your time management these step-back periods will help you regain perspective.

- The more reactive, event driven and chaotic your world is, the greater is the need to plan and review those plans regularly.

Part 3

Points for action

What have been the major learning points from this part of the book?
1.
2.
3.
4.
5.

What specific actions do you intend to take to develop your time management effectiveness? Select no more than *five* actions and list in priority sequence. Prioritise based on the positive impact you believe the action will have. Commit to timescales – when you intend to implement the action.
1.
2.
3.
4.
5.

PART 4

Staying focused

CHAPTER 11

So why does it all go wrong?

You are a planned and organised person. You have a time system, you are disciplined, spend time each day reprioritising as required. However, you still find that you are short of time, that you are being taken away from your plans, and that your priorities are pushed to one side. Why? The simple answer is of course the unexpected. If we just accept this we will not move forward and be able to take control of our time. The unexpected is too simple an answer. We need to understand the root causes, and what the other factors are that impact on our plans. In this chapter we will identify what these factors are. Then we can move on to look at some of the solutions, again remembering that there is no magic wand.

Below I have summarised what I believe are the principal causes for it all going wrong. I am sure that you will be able to relate to some or indeed all of them. You may well find that some of these are linked, and that the time problems you are experiencing are caused by a combination of them. I ask you not to get depressed as you read through the list, and not to think that trying to manage time is all in vain! I am confident that there are answers to most of these issues, or at least actions that you can take to improve a current situation.

There are simply too many things to do

Let's start with the difficult one first. We all face this situation from time to time but if you are faced with overload for the majority of the time then this is a serious situation. We have already discussed prioritising and rescheduling but if every day produces the same level of overload then all you are doing is moving the problem, not working towards a solution.

Other people are poor time managers

Have you ever thought why that particular work colleague is always coming to you with the 'this is really urgent can you do it now' request? Why is it always urgent? The answer may be that they are not planning medium and long term, they are waiting until actions become urgent and then reacting. In most businesses and in most job roles there is some interdependency. For example, you may need input and information from someone in a different department before you can complete an action. Likewise, other people will require cooperation from you if they are to complete their tasks and projects. This is a key point. We impact on and are impacted on by others.

Everything takes longer than you thought it would

This seems to be one of the fundamental rules of life, and I believe that it is one of the significant reasons for plans falling apart. The effect of one task for which you had planned 30 minutes taking, say, 20% longer would not seem to be significant. After all, six minutes is hardly significant. However, if this happens to all deadlines, particularly for a complex task of, say, half a day, then the impact becomes significant.

My priorities are not their priorities

In a business context, at a company level all employees have common goals in that everybody is working to support the organisation's goals and strategy. However, in detail, your priorities may be different to those of a colleague in another department or team. Therefore when you approach someone asking them to devote some of their time to one of your priorities, they may be reluctant to agree because they are busy working on a different priority. Of course, the same is true in reverse. I am sure you have experienced the type of interruption in which you think that you cannot be really bothered with this because it is not important. It may not be to you, but it may well be very important to the other person. This is not to say that one person's set of priorities is right and the other person's is wrong. They are just different.

Most people are keen to please

We can all think of people we have met, in work or social life, who go out of their way not to help, not to say yes, to generally not cooperate. However, in my experience most people are keen and willing to please. This is a tribute to the human race in general, and no one should have a goal of changing the good in fellow human beings! However, in time management terms this willingness can be a problem. Certainly an over-willingness can result in unrealistic commitments being made, and then compounded because other people's plans are based on them. This is a delicate issue, as clearly converting people to being unhelpful in the cause of better time management is not a solution.

The goal posts keep moving

Many of us live our lives at a fast pace. The companies we work for are operating in fast-moving markets which are increasingly competitive. The strategy for yesterday may not be the right one for next week. We are living in a world where it seems that the priorities keep changing. Some of the changes are legitimate; others are not, but merely the result of a knee-jerk reaction to the latest crisis.

Conclusions

The above issues describe the real world for a lot of us most of the time. These issues disrupt our plans, take us away from our priorities. What we have discussed so far is intended to help us be focused, planned and organised. We now move on to how we can stay focused in the light of the realities.

Before moving on to the next chapter take a few moments to review the list above. If you feel that there are other issues not listed, issues that are relevant to you as they are factors that cause you to lose your focus and threaten your priorities, make a note of them below. You can review them later, and look at some of the solutions that we have discussed.

1.
2.
3.
4.
5.

CHAPTER 12

Behaviour and communication

Time planning and time management would be very simple and straightforward if you had total control of everything in your life, both in and out of work. The reality is that you have to work and live with others, and acknowledge their responsibilities and priorities. We have already discussed interdependency. You are dependent on others for the achievement of your goals, others are dependent on you. As we have said, no one is an island.

In terms of staying focused, let us return to our earlier analogy of your goals being your destination. The tasks and activities you complete are the are the means of getting there. Your goals may legitimately change, in which case you re-plan your tasks, effectively re-chart your course and set off in a new direction. Your goals may not change but as you are travelling along the road to your goals outside influences will have an impact, making demands on you that will divert you from that course. Some of those demands will be valid, which will result in you taking a diversion from your set course. Others will not.

These factors – the interdependency, and the demands that will divert you from your course – mean that staying focused is, in reality, a balancing act. If your goals have not changed you need to maintain your course towards your destination. However, you must accept some diversions while rejecting others. The planning and organisational skills we have discussed so far will help you track your course, capture the diversions, and re-plan as required, but on their own they are not enough to ensure that you stay focused.

Behavioural and communication skills are required, because staying focused involves dealing with the *facts* of the situation and the *people* involved. To recap:

- The priorities that other people have may well be different to yours.

- Their priorities are as valid to them as yours are to you.

- Others have a dependency on you, you have a dependency on others.

- The demands on your time being made by others may be legitimate, as these actions constitute a higher priority than your planned actions.

This means that you cannot simply hold on to your plans and automatically block requests and demands from others. However, you have a right to defend and to hold on to your priorities and protect your time from demands that are not legitimate. There are two challenges.

1. To continue to focus on the priorities, accepting that those priorities may have changed from those that you had planned.

2. To maintain the relationship. This will be especially important when you have made the decision that your original priorities assume a greater importance than that represented by the unscheduled demand on your time – you are therefore rejecting a request from someone else.

In this chapter we are focusing on solutions to the second challenge, that of relationship management. How you manage the dialogue of discussing and agreeing the priorities will have a direct impact on your ability to stay focused, as well as determining future relationships.

Let me give you an example. Your boss has come to you and requested that you provide a detailed report by the end of the day. This is an unexpected request – it is not normally part of your role to produce this report, and you are very busy working on a proposal for an important customer for which the deadline is today. In your opinion the work for the customer represents a higher priority than producing an internal report. If you handle this situation in the wrong way you face three potential negative consequences:

- you damage your relationship with your boss;

- your boss can order you as a last resort; and

- you fail to supply the important customer with the information that they need.

You may have logic on your side, but we all know that when two people are under pressure facts and rational thought become blurred! *How* you handle the communication will be all important if the right decision for both parties, and in this example the business, is to be made. This example relates to the work environment, but we face exactly the same issues in social and family life. The solutions we will be discussing are equally valid in work and out of work situations.

In the work context where are these unscheduled demands on your time likely to come from?

1. *Your manager, or someone senior to you in the organisation.*
    In my experience most people find this the most difficult situation to challenge. 'How can I say no to my boss?' is a frequent question. I agree this is not easy, and the level of difficulty or ease will be determined by the relationship you have. However, if you are going to hold on to your priorities you must be prepared to challenge. The word challenge does imply 'combat'. This is why the behaviour used in any such dialogue must be such that reasoned dialogue rather than challenge comes across.

2. *Customers.* Customers are the lifeblood for any business, and as such an unscheduled demand from a customer will assume a higher priority than any other tasks that you are working on. For many people working in sales or customer services, responding to their customers' requests is the core purpose of their job. However, what do you do in the situation where a number of customers are making demands on your time, all at the same time, all with the same urgency? You cannot satisfy all of them. You have to make decisions. This will involve saying to some of them that you cannot meet their requests within the timescales demanded. Again, how you handle that communication is vital. Handle it incorrectly and the customer may not accept your case and simply demand you do what they want now. We all live in competitive worlds so maintaining a customer relationship when you are effectively saying to them I cannot do what you want now is key.

3. *Colleagues and team members.* You may not feel the same level of pressure when questioning a demand on your time from a colleague as you would from a manager or a customer. The implications would appear to be less severe! However, we have discussed the interdependency that exists between job roles, so even if someone does not have the right of veto over you, maintaining harmony and a good working relationship is still important.

Demands on your time will come from other parties – for example, strategic partners and suppliers. The potential issues will be as in the examples above. I will not attempt to detail the implications of challenging demands on your time in your out of work life, because of the possible variables depending on your particular circumstances, though these can include time demands from your partner, children, parents, friends, etc.

The issues and challenges are the same regardless of the situation. If you are going to hold on to your priorities you may have to say no to demands from others on your time.

Before we move on to discuss the behaviours that will help you manage these situations effectively so that there are positive outcomes for all concerned, let me make three points. I stress that these points are important in setting the context for how and why we challenge demands on our time, and how we respond.

- I have already stated my belief that most people are keen to please. While we can all think of exceptions to this I believe that this view represents most people most of the time. I have said that an over-eagerness to please can be in conflict with staying focused and holding on to priorities. Neither I nor anybody else should try and change people from having this positive human trait of helpfulness into people who automatically say no to a request. Therefore, if there is an unscheduled demand on your time, but it does not represent a threat to your schedule, then agree to it and do it. You only need to challenge a request on your time if that request threatens your priorities and their timescales. In other words, the potential conflict only arises if there is not enough time to complete everything in the time available. This is where the prioritisation system described in Chapter 8 can help. In summary, do not become a 'no, I will not do this' person!

- When you are rejecting a request, for the legitimate reason that the tasks you are working on represent a greater priority than that of the unscheduled demand, you are not saying 'no, full stop'. You are saying, 'I cannot do this at the moment, for valid reasons'. Again this is important, as the issue is now only one of when. A timescale which is acceptable to both of you needs to be negotiated. We will cover the how of this later in this chapter.

- Balance your picture with the big picture. This is about balancing your priorities with the priorities of others. In discussing the issues in staying focused I highlighted that one of the problems is that people have different priorities. I am defining the big picture as the common goals and priorities. In the work context people have their own functional priorities, but they all should be focused on achievement of the corporate and overall business goals. This is the common ground. So when faced with a demand on your time, which will take you away from your functional priorities, you need to step back and consider the contribution this unscheduled task represents to the overall objectives.

In summary, staying focused is not as simple as following a set of rules and procedures – it requires judgement, and a perspective of the big picture. This reinforces the need for communication and behavioural skills to stay focused.

An effective communication model

'Be tough on the issues not on the people.' This relates back to the statement made in the Tenth Commandment for time management, be ruthless with time and gracious with people.

You may be familiar with a number of communication models from training and development programmes you have attended during your career or from previous reading that you have done. In this section of the chapter I will describe the principles of the assertion model, and then illustrate how applying assertion will help you stay focused as well as retain and develop relationships.

The model is outlined in Table 12.1 and defines any behaviour as falling into one of three categories, one of which will be the most effective behaviour for the vast majority of situations.

Table 12.1 The principles of the assertion model

Aggressive behaviour

Characteristics of aggressive behaviour are as follows:
- High levels of emotions are displayed.
- Not prepared to listen to the views and positions of others.
- An unwillingness to consider the priorities of others.
- A determination to win by holding on to priorities.

Non-assertive behaviour

Characteristics of non-assertive behaviour are as follows:
- A lack of confidence or conviction is displayed.
- Not prepared to state and to hold on to priorities.
- There is a desire to avoid issues and conflicts.

Assertive behaviour

Characteristics of assertive behaviour are as follows:
- Being clear about one's own priorities and being prepared to state them.
- Being logical and rational, avoiding displays of emotion.
- Listening to other people's views and their priorities.
- Being prepared to discuss an issue to arrive at a win–win situation.

From the descriptions given in the table it is clear what is the most effective style in resolving demands on your time and reconciling priorities. The use of aggressive behaviour will mean that you will stay focused but what will the cost be in terms of relationships and understanding the big picture priorities? If you use non-assertive behaviour you will avoid conflict and be seen as an accommodating person but the cost will be a loss of your priorities and the pressure of too much to do in too little time. On the other hand, practising and developing assertive behaviour will result in:

- you staying focused on your priorities;

- you responding to changing priorities when the changes are valid;

- you contributing to the big picture goals as well as your own;

- you maintaining and building relationships.

What is assertion?

What is involved in staying focused and holding on to your priorities, and making the correct decisions about changes to those priorities when faced with unscheduled demands on your time from others? There are a number of stages and factors to work through and consider:

- What is the nature of the interruption, the demand on my time?

- Does it represent a greater priority than my planned tasks?

- What is the actual deadline?
- Is this a task I should be involving myself in?
- How long will it take to complete, and what is involved?
- Can I fit this task in without disrupting my schedule or putting my current deadlines at risk?
- If there is a conflict – there is not enough time to complete everything – what agreement can be made with the other party?

In short, you have to have a dialogue with the person who is placing demands on your time if you are to reach the right decision. Are you thinking that this sounds time consuming? I promise you it does not take as much time as you may think, and we must keep in mind the principle that you need to invest time to make time in the future. Also, what are the alternatives? You can resort to aggression, which may give you a short-term win at the expense of others, with the risk that the request you rejected assumes a greater priority for you and the business as a whole. Non-assertion is the non-discussion option as well – you simply accept every request and demand placed on you. The result will be a lack of control, loss of your priorities, overload and eventually not delivering on any of your commitments satisfactorily. The answer is to develop assertion as the behaviour which will help you manage time demands, requests for your time and the shifting of priorities.

What does assertion involve?

I have defined assertion, and what it means at a broad level. Now let us look at what assertion involves.

Asking questions, to gain a clear understanding of what the request is and the implications of the request. You will need to determine the nature of the task, what priority it has, how long it will take you to complete, and when it needs to be completed.

Active listening, because there is no point in asking questions if you are not able or prepared to listen to the answers. The answers to the questions will enable you to discuss and agree a way forward, a solution.

- *Openly discussing the situation*, so that you can arrive at a joint course of action. This could involve questioning the deadline, discussing if the deadlines could be pushed back, and possibly arriving at a compromise solution with which you can both live.

- *Negotiating a deadline*, which is a follow-on from the discussion, where the facts have been clarified. Remember the tendency people to have to state an urgent deadline without much thought. It is often possible to move a deadline.

- *Signalling that you understand* the pressures and priorities of the other person. Understanding is quite different to agreement. Using language like 'I appreciate your problem',

'I can see why this is important to you', 'I would really like to help' will demonstrate that you are taking a positive balanced view and not just rejecting a request out of hand.

- *Rejecting a demand*, if necessary, remembering the rule, 'be tough on the issues not on the people'. If a demand on your time is not legitimate because it represents a lower priority than the work you are engaged in and there is no possibility that both tasks can be completed, you have a right to reject the request. Focus on the facts, and keep emotion out of the discussion. When rejecting a demand, give a reason for the rejection. If you are rejecting the stipulated timescale, so are saying 'I will do it but I cannot do it now', then make this clear.

To help you understand the context for these guidelines think of a recent example where someone was making a request for your time, or you were making a demand on someone else's time. This could be in a work or out of work situation. Consider what the outcomes would be given one or both parties responding aggressively, non-assertively and finally assertively. Ask yourself if the actual outcome was satisfactory, and if the situation could have been more positive if the principles of assertion had been applied.

Conclusions

While I can give you examples of assertive behaviour as I have done above, the written word, in itself, cannot provide the total behaviour and how it will be received. I need to relate back to 'mindset' again. The underpinning requirement for demonstrating assertive behaviour is conviction and confidence. In the context of staying focused this means having the conviction that the priorities you are working on are valid and having the confidence to protect them when it is valid to do so. If you apply the principles covered in the previous parts of this book – getting focused on your goals, organising your self so you work on the actions to achieve them – then you will have the conviction that your priorities are valid.

Being able to communicate in a positive confident manner is important in business and life terms generally and is not restricted to protecting your time. In this chapter I have sought to demonstrate how these communication principles can be applied to protecting your time.

To summarise, so far in this book we have discussed getting focused, getting organised and, in this chapter, staying focused. Of the three I believe that staying focused is the most difficult. In the other stages you have a high degree of control as you are effectively defining your goals (the destination) and then planning your actions (the route, the road map). Staying focused involves maintaining your course in the light of the unplanned events and crises (the diversions) that you will experience. So you have less control than in the planning stages. Also, getting focused and getting organised involve using planning and organising skills, which are, in a sense, definable, and processes and tools such as those that we have discussed can help. Staying focused is highly dependent on behaviour and communication, and behavioural science is a less exact discipline. Some readers will already have developed the skills of assertive behaviour so staying focused will not represent such a challenge. Those who need to develop these skills will probably find this a greater challenge than mastering the planning and organisation elements. I state this not from the point of view of a defeatist or pessimist, since developing communication and behavioural effectiveness can be achieved by everyone. It is a statement of what I believe is reality, based on my experience working with many people on developing time management effectiveness over a number of years. I am also sending a signal that much of the effort you may put into getting focused and organised will be diluted if you do not put at least as much into developing the skills required to keep you focused.

PART 4

Staying focused – key messages and action plan

- The challenges to staying focused are numerous – too many things to do, other people's poor time management, differing priorities, things taking longer than planned, changing goal posts, an over-eagerness to please. These challenges must be managed.
- You have to work with others, there is an interdependency. This means that you must manage the facts of the situation and the people involved.
- You have a right to hold on to your priorities, but you have to recognise that those priorities may change for valid reasons.
- Staying focused is dependent on behavioural and communication skills.
- Assertion is the positive behaviour to develop.

- Assertion involves asking questions, listening, discussing options, negotiating deadlines, displaying understanding, and when rejecting requests providing a rationale.
- In rejecting requests you are not necessarily saying no, but no not now.

Part 4

Points for action

What have been the major learning points from this part of the book?
1.
2.
3.
4.
5.

What specific actions do you intend to take to develop your time management effectiveness? Select no more than *five* actions and list in priority sequence. Prioritise based on the positive impact you believe the action will have. Commit to timescales – when you intend to implement the action.
1.
2.
3.
4.
5.

PART 5

Specific time management techniques

Introduction

In Parts 2 to 4 I have provided you with an overall framework for developing your time effectiveness, under the following topics:

- *Getting focused*, which is about being clear about your goals, what you want to achieve, in both your in work and out of work time.

- *Getting organised*, which deals with prioritising, introducing a system and being disciplined in its use, so that you are able to focus on the tasks and activities that will be high contributors to the achievement of your goals.

- *Staying focused*, which primarily covers the behavioural skills to enable you to manage the unexpected demands on your time at both a factual and relationship level.

In each part the key relevant skills and techniques have been discussed. For example, in 'Getting focused' we covered smart goals; in 'Getting organised' I suggested prioritising using the ABC–123 system; in 'Staying focused' I introduced you to the principles of assertive behaviour. So, all of the skill and technique discussions have been specific to a stage in the three-point model.

In Part 5 I will be covering a broader range of time management skills and techniques that can be used to develop your overall time effectiveness. While they are not directly linked to any stage in the model, each will have varying degrees of relevance to individual readers, based on specific job roles and life styles. I suggest you view this list of skills and techniques as a menu which you can select from. For example, if you are never or only rarely involved in attending or arranging meetings then reading the chapter on 'the meetings myth' may be a low priority for you. If you work as part of a virtual team and spend much of your time working from a home base you will find the chapter on 'the e-world issues' highly relevant.

I believe that all of the skills and techniques discussed will add value in developing your time skills. I suggest that you practise the art of prioritising by deciding on the sequence in which you will read the chapters based on the importance and relevance each has for you. The table below will help you prioritise. Although there are twelve chapters altogether I strongly suggest you read Chapter 13 – 'Be in tune with your body' – first, regardless of how you prioritise the other eleven. My reason is that the learning points from this chapter may well help when reading the others.

Chapter		Sequence
13	Be in tune with your body	1
14	Delegating	
15	The meetings myth	
16	Think team	
17	The e-world issues	
18	Be decisive – go for the hard tasks	
19	Task batching	
20	No interrupt zones	
21	Realistic time estimating	
22	Travel and away time	
23	Be creative as well as corrective	
24	Managing stress	

CHAPTER 13

Be in tune with your body

The energy curve

No, I have not lost direction and moved from time management to providing medical advice! Let me relay to you a personal experience from many years ago to illustrate the link between being in tune with your body and time management.

I had applied for and been accepted for a job in the industrial sales division of a major company in the fast-moving consumer goods sector. I had been interviewed by: the sales director, an HR manager and a regional sales manager who would be my direct line manager. The interview was in two stages, and both had been held early afternoon. The interviews went well, and I felt that good relationships had developed even in the short space of the interview.

It is now four weeks later, early Monday morning around 7.00 a.m. in a hotel. I am just about to start a three-week induction programme at the company's head office. I had travelled up the night before, and my new boss, the regional sales manager, one of the interview team, had arranged to meet me for breakfast.

Now I am the sort of person who is up with the larks and am, for example, quite happy to be travelling at 5.00 a.m. in the morning, particularly in the summer. So, in meeting with my new manager, I was my usual high-energy self, and of course I was eager to create a good impression with my new boss. Something had gone wrong! He was decidedly unhappy, and every attempt I made at conversation was met by a short response before he buried himself back in his newspaper. What had I done? Was he having second thoughts about recruiting me? Could this be the shortest career move ever?

Let me now fast forward to 8.00 p.m. the same day. I am back in the hotel. So is my new boss. We are having dinner. He is animated, eager to hear how my first day was, asking me about he holiday I had just returned from, explaining the career opportunities in the company. I left him the bar at 11.00 p.m., where he had met with some other people in the company who had just checked in. I wandered back to my bedroom wondering if I my new boss was suffering from acute schizophrenia. Breakfast tomorrow would help me check out my theory.

In fact my boss was quite sane, and the answer, with the benefit of experience and additional insights into behaviour, is obvious – we had different energy curves. An *energy curve* plots the peaks and troughs in your energy and therefore effectiveness at various points throughout the day. In broad terms my boss would be described as a late energy person, whereas I am an early energy person. We have all experienced people with different energy curves. I am sure that there are people you have worked with who, like my boss of many years ago, do not seem to come alive till late morning, but will then display high energy through to midnight. Similarly you will know people who have completed five reports and designed three presentations by the time we mere mortals arrive at the office.

The labels early and late energy are too simplistic, yet they do describe in broad terms at what point in the day individuals have maximum and minimum energy. To give you a more detailed example, my energy curve is as follows.

- Early morning through to lunchtime is my maximum energy period.

- From 1.00 p.m. through to 3.00 p.m. this levels out.

- The trough comes between 4.00 p.m. and 7.00 p.m.

- From between 7.00 p.m. and 9.30 p.m. is a return to medium energy level.

Now I do not claim to have scientifically carried out this analysis! Given knowledge of the energy curve I have been more aware of the peaks and troughs throughout the day, and I have the feedback from colleagues. You can imagine how I felt when I was asked by a client to facilitate a series of training workshops that would start at 4.30 p.m. and finish at 8.30 p.m., and then a normal 9.00 a.m. to 5.00 p.m. agenda on day two? Of course you can be engaged in intense work during your low energy period of the day – it is just more difficult. No two people are the same. For some people, the gap between the peaks and the troughs may be less significant than for others. There is no right or wrong, good or bad. While you can discipline yourself to maintain a constant work rate throughout the day you will not be able to fundamentally change your energy curve – it is a given, it is part of you. You will be more effective during some parts of the day than others.

Your energy curve and time effectiveness

How can an awareness of your energy curve help you develop your time effectiveness? I am sure that you are aware of the fact that you have high and low energy periods during the day. Have you ever thought about it in relation to time management and considered it when planning your time? Given that you will be more effective at certain times of the day you can select tasks to coincide with your high and your low points. For example, if you are an early energy person schedule complex tasks, jobs for which you need periods of concentration, for first thing in the morning. To link back to the task categories we discussed in Part 3, 'future' tasks, which may, for example involve project work, would be best tackled in a high energy period. Managing 'today' tasks, which would typically involve more routine functions with which you are more familiar, can be scheduled for a time in your low energy period, say mid afternoon. Late energy people would plan so that the complex tasks are scheduled for mid–late afternoon when they are coming alive.

It will not always be possible to schedule tasks in synchronisation with your energy curve, because in the real world you work with other people and have to accommodate their schedules. Also, it is not so simplistic as merely task labelling. If you are a late energy person when would you schedule meetings? The answer is that it depends on the nature of the meeting. A routine departmental progress report meeting could be handled during a relatively low energy time. However, a creative brainstorming meeting to determine product strategy for the next five years would be better scheduled for a high energy period! The key is to think in terms of complexity and levels of concentration needed rather than in terms of categories of tasks. For example, writing one report may be straightforward, requiring relatively little mental effort, whereas another report may stretch the mind.

I have acknowledged that for some planning you are dependent on other people; however, planned tasks which can be scheduled and only involve you can be allocated time considering your relative energy levels at times of the day. To return to other people, given that your colleagues will have different energy curves to you, how do you agree times to schedule tasks where you have to work with them? Of course, there is no simple answer to this. However, if you are working with the same people on a frequent basis you can establish the overlap times where you are all at a reasonable, if not peak, energy level. As a general rule, if you are working with colleagues with different energy curves, schedule joint working and meeting times for late morning or late afternoon. There is an element of compromise here but at these times all of you will be at least at an acceptable if not maximum energy level. You can all address the complex, high concentration tasks with a joint maximum effectiveness.

Does this sound as if it is going to take a lot of analysis time? Again we come back to investing time to make time. Step back and consider when you embarked on a complex task and it felt that you had made no headway. It may have been that you encountered a number of unplanned crises so you became distracted. Or it could be that you tried to tackle a hard task at the wrong time for you! Ask yourself the following questions:

- When do I think my high energy levels are high? If you are not sure ask your colleagues or your partner. They can probably tell you.

- Recall situations when you were effective at completing the demanding tasks. At what times in the day did you complete them?

- When are your low energy times? Can you think of specific situations where you are frankly not as effective as you think you could be.

The answers to these questions will give you some clues as to where you fit on the energy curve. As with most of the learning points we have covered, do not see the conclusions as imposing rules on you. Simply consider when you are at your best and at your least effective, and plan accordingly. At the same time, you cannot cater for the unplanned! You will have to deal with high-demand, complex, non-planned tasks when they do not coincide with your high energy times – this is reality. However, by planning what you can plan, and wherever possible scheduling tasks in line with your energy curve, you will maximise your effectiveness.

Overall energy levels

Finally, do not confuse the energy curve with absolute energy levels. It is a fact that some people have higher energy levels than others. I have said that your energy curve is a given. Is your absolute energy level also a given? I do not think it is. For example, by achieving a work–life balance you will suffer less stress and be able to improve your overall effectiveness. Let me end by giving you my personal experience of this. I am, as I have said, an early energy person. By 4.00 p.m. I am at my lowest level. Now, this may sound incongruous, but if I am working on a project where I have some flexible working time I will go the gym for a one-hour workout at around this time. The result is that I can return to work re-energised and be more productive than if I had not taken the break.

These are key learning points – the work–life balance is important, energy levels at the mental and physical levels are different, and physical exercise can influence and improve energy levels back at work.

CHAPTER 14
===

Delegating

Firstly, I will provide some definitions of delegation, then we will see how it relates to developing your time effectiveness and look at some of the perceived common barriers there are to delegating. Then I will provide some guidelines to help you identify your own delegation opportunities, remembering the objective is to improve your time effectiveness.

What is delegation?

A general perception of delegation is that it is a process whereby a manger allocates tasks to members of staff. These may be tasks that the manager has historically completed, or new tasks that have been given to the manager who subsequently decides to pass them on to a staff member. There may be some cynicism where some mangers are perceived to be abdicating their responsibilities by transferring a heavy workload to someone else. However, there is a big difference between legitimate delegation and simply reducing your workload by overloading others. Later in this chapter we will discuss the rules of delegation.

While the classic view of delegation as a manager allocating tasks to a subordinate is valid we need to think of it in a broader context. Many organisations no longer have fixed structures with line managers and staff. More and more people work in fluid teams which are often project based. Increasingly people work remotely in virtual teams, and some can be working in more than one team simultaneously. These more flexible structures change the sense of what we mean by delegation.

In the context of time management, and appreciating that many people do not work in highly structured functional groups, delegation is about the following:

- Defining how you, your colleagues and team members can be most effective in terms of use of time, and then agreeing who is picking up responsibility for various aspects of the workload.

- Seeing delegation as potentially a '360 degree' process. The traditional perception is that delegation is one way, from manager to a member of staff. However, tasks can be delegated to team members, peers and also to more senior people.

Barriers to delegation

Many people, whether they work in a traditional or less structured work environment, are uncomfortable about delegating tasks. There are a number of possible reasons.

- *I am the best person to do the job.* This may be true, in the sense that you are the most experienced and currently you are the most effective in completing it. On the other hand, there may be other people in the organisation who are just as capable. A key question you must ask is 'what level of contribution will completion of this task make to my goals?' If it is a low contributor, should you be spending time on it? Is the task more relevant to someone else's goals?

- *By the time I have explained what to do I could have done it myself.* This is aligned with the first point, since you may be the fastest, the most effective. The question is, over time, can someone else become as effective as you and take the task over? We are back, yet again, to the principle of investing time to make time. Investing time now to brief and train someone else will free you up in the medium and long term to focus on bigger priorities.

- *Fear of losing control.* This as an understandable fear, as by delegating a task to someone else you will not be so close to that aspect of the operation. For many there is a comfort in being involved in the detail of everything! If a task represents a high contribution to your goals and it is essential that you are closely involved in it then it should not be delegated. However, you must ask yourself the question, 'can I do everything?' If the answer comes back no, then you will need to make some decisions, and prioritise. Delegation is a possible solution.

- *What if it all goes wrong?* This is linked in with the third point in that if you are in control you feel there is the best chance of the task being completed correctly. The other fear is that if it goes wrong you will be blamed, even though it was outside of your control. Of course, you must be confident that the person you are delegating to has the necessary knowledge and skill to complete the job. But there is no such thing as a risk-free decision.

- *I like doing it myself.* Can we have another honesty session? I think that most of us are guilty of holding on to jobs that we like doing! The sort of task that you feel comfortable with, you took it on some time ago and it now represents part of your habit. Yes, three years ago it was absolutely relevant to your goals, but since then you have changed your role, possibly been promoted. Is the task completion still a high contributor to the achievement of your job goals? However, we are allowed some weakness! If you like doing it, even though you acknowledge that it is not a high contributor, as long as it is not threatening the completion of your real priorities, then fine. One day, though, you may have to acknowledge the issue and give it up.

- *There is no one to delegate to!* Most organisations today run lean, so most people have a full set of commitments. This is a genuine constraint. I have already said that delegation is not abdication, simply trying to clear your desk at the expense of someone else. Therefore, for some people delegation opportunities may be limited. However this should not stop you from carrying out an analysis of your tasks to identify what possibilities there are to re-distribute tasks and workload with the objective of improving your time effectiveness without impacting on the effectiveness of others.

Although we are discussing delegation specifically in relation to improved time management I would like to highlight the additional potential benefits to the organisation, and to the people in the business of delegation. Delegation does provide genuine opportunities for people to develop. People can learn new skills by attending training courses or self-study but one of the most effective learning mechanisms is having the opportunity to be involved in additional jobs. People are eager to learn, so being asked to take on an additional responsibility will often be viewed positively. Even with a busy schedule there is usually some opportunity to stretch, given sound organisational and prioritisation skills.

To develop the previous point, saying to someone that you would like them to take over, effectively, part of your job can be motivational. From their perspective, what are you saying? That you trust them, that you believe that they are capable of taking on more responsibility, that you believe that they are capable of more. Consider the different perceptions. You may be feeling guilty if you think you may be overloading people with work, while a member of your team may be de-motivated if they feel that they are not being involved in more and different aspects of the role because you do not trust their abilities. There has to be a balance, as it is also de-motivating if you feel work is being dumped on you and that you are being taken for granted.

Delegation can reduce risk and dependency for the organisation. If you are the only person who is able to complete a particular task, what happens when you are away on holiday, ill or overloaded with other priorities? Delegation spreads knowledge and ability across a team and creates a better balance. So, applying delegation can have a number of positive outcomes.

We will now return to delegation in the context of improving time effectiveness we will now look at how you can analyse your tasks and workload to arrive at delegation opportunities.

Task analysis, delegation opportunities

In carrying out this analysis it useful to refer back to the task categories I introduced to you in Part 3, 'Getting organised'. To recap, these were 'now', 'future' and unplanned tasks. As a general guide, but by no means a rule, 'future' tasks will not be those that you would consider delegating. They should represent a high priority and be high contributors to your goals as they are concerned with developing rather than maintaining. Within the other two categories there will be a range of tasks, some of which will represent delegation opportunities.

Table 14.1 categorises your workload from four different points of view in terms of possible delegation. As a result of such an analysis you should be able to define some delegation opportunities, some of which you may be able to action immediately. You may also want to highlight opportunities for the mid term – for tasks where currently members of your team or colleagues do not have the experience or knowledge to take them over, but with some training and coaching this would be possible.

Let me also restate the point that delegation is not just available to line managers who have reporting staff to whom they can delegate. Delegation should be seen in a broader context of who has the necessary skill and knowledge, who has the available time, and to whose goals the task is most relevant.

Table 14.1 Work categories and delegation

Must do	These are tasks that have a high contribution to the achievement of your goals and require your experience and skill to complete them. There may be some questions of confidentiality, which is another reason why they could not be delegated. All of these tasks would fall into the 'A' category of importance.
Should do	These are tasks with a mid to high importance ranking which therefore represent significant contributors to the achievement of your goals. It is therefore unlikely that you would consider delegating them. These tasks fall into the 'A' and 'B' importance categories.
Could do	These are mid level contributors and would generally be prioritised as 'B' tasks. In addition, some category 'C' tasks could be included provided they do not involve a high percentage of your available time. However, you should consider delegation possibilities for some of these tasks.
Should not do	These are category 'C' tasks and are therefore low contributors to the achievement of your goals. You should minimise the time you spend on them and seriously look at delegation opportunities. In reality you may need to hold on to some of them because of the lack of time others will have to take them over.

In Tables 14.2 and 14.3 I have provided examples of charts that you can use to draw up your jobs/tasks list, putting them in one of the four categories – must do, should do, could do, should not do. I have added a final column to indicate the tasks which someone else should be able to complete in your absence – labelled 'cover needed'.

Table 14.3 can then be used to log your delegation opportunities. Use the columns under the staff member/colleague heading to indicate, using their initials, who you may be able to delegate that specific task to. You may, for example, wish to delegate the task to two people, each person completing a part. In the 'Reasons' column state the main reason for your decision, for example 'Cover needed in my absence', 'Development opportunity', etc.

So, using Table 14.2, draw up a list of the tasks you carry out in your job. Against each, tick whether it is a must do/should do/could do/should not do. Put a tick in the 'cover' column if the tasks need delegating to someone while you are away.

Then transfer the jobs you have identified for possible delegation to Table 14.3.

Table 14.2 Job categories and delegation

Jobs	Must do	Should do	Could do	Should not do	Cover needed

Table 14.3 Delegation chart

Tasks	Staff member/Colleague								Reasons

Guidelines for effective delegation

I have already highlighted the difference between abdication and delegation. To delegate effectively you need to follow a set of simple guidelines. If you do not follow these the chances are that the whole exercise will cost you time!

There are six guidelines to follow:

1. You need to provide a clear briefing in terms of what is involved, what is required and by when.

2. The person you are considering delegating a task to must have the necessary knowledge and skills for the job. If you believe that they would be capable in the future, then you need to go through a coaching programme before you hand the task over.

3. When you have delegated a task you must leave the person to get on with it. If you are constantly checking and looking over their shoulder you may as well do the job yourself.

4. As a balance to point 3 you should be available to provide assistance when requested.

5. Agree with the person you have delegated to a review time to answer any questions that they may have and to make sure that they are approaching the task correctly. This is preferable to reaching the required completion date to find that they misunderstood and have got it wrong.

6. Finally, you must accept that accountability cannot be delegated. Even though someone else is now responsible for completing the task you are still responsible for its successful completion on time. This may sound unfair, but it was your decision to delegate the task.

Summary

- Delegation is a major opportunity to improve your time effectiveness as it releases you to concentrate on your priorities.
- Think of delegation in a broader context than a manager delegating to a member of staff.
- Generally you should not consider delegating your 'future' tasks.
- Do not confuse delegation with abdication.
- In addition to improving time effectiveness there are other positive outcomes for the business and the people in the business, for example, providing development opportunities.
- Follow the six-point guidelines for effective delegation.

CHAPTER 15

The meetings myth

If you polled a sample of people and asked about their attitude to meetings what sort of response would you get? I believe that the views expressed would be generally negative and even cynical, with a conclusion that they soak up a lot of valuable time unnecessarily. Then why is it that meetings retain their position as a fundamental part of business life? I am sure, like me, you know people who seem to spend the majority of lives in meetings. Are they being effective? Are they making best use of their time? What are the alternatives to the seemingly endless rounds of meetings?

Of course it is wrong to say that all meetings are bad and a waste of time. Business is about relationships, people working together in teams, working on projects. Even with the technology available to us we still need to meet colleagues, customers, suppliers, team members and business partners. Some would argue that meetings are justified simply because they bring people together. I can, in certain circumstances, given specific conditions, buy into that view. However, there are some organisations where the knee-jerk reaction to any problem is to gather a crowd to attend a meeting. However, as with most things in life, it is a question of balance.

In the context of time management, where the objective is to maximise your own and others' time effectiveness, we need to address two questions:

1. Is a meeting necessary? There may be other ways of achieving the same outcome in less time and at less cost. If you were to analyse the cost of a meeting involving, say, five people for half a day the answer would be quite staggering in terms of salary and overhead costs, travel cost, etc. The value of the outcome would need to be weighed against this cost.

2. If the answer is yes, a meeting is the only way to achieve what you want to achieve, then we need to ensure that it is organised and structured in such a way that it minimises the impact on people's time and achieves an output. A well organised meeting can be very productive. A poorly organised meeting frustrates people and wastes the resources of the business.

Do we need a meeting?

Let me provide you with two mini case studies to introduce the debate on the options to meetings.

Case study 1

I was working with a client on a project where we were required to restructure some of their current training courses. At a meeting with one of the people in the client's project team I had picked up the action to produce an initial design within the following two weeks. She then suggested a further meeting for two weeks time with her and a colleague to review our initial work and decide what, if any, amendments would be needed. Without really thinking it through I suggested a date, she agreed, and the arrangement was made. This was the first learning point. I had automatically said yes to the meeting without thinking through the options.

Back in the office I stepped back and thought through the logistics. I could produce the initial design and e-mail the report to the client within ten days. What was the logic of spending between six to seven hours driving (the round trip would involve nearly 500 miles!) for possibly a two-hour meeting, when the initial design we had produced may require no amendments? My suggestion to the client was that I would e-mail the report, give them three days to study it, and then arrange an early morning conference call to get their feedback to establish what amendments they needed and to agree the next project stages. My rationale was that after the call I would have the day to action what was required rather than spend the time on the 250-mile return trip. The conference call took half an hour, the amendments they required were minimal and I was able to complete them by the end of the day. I made most effective use of my time, helped my clients make most effective use of their time, and saved them money as we were able to progress the project at less than the agreed fees.

The relationship was already established, the objectives of the project were agreed, so a face-to-face meeting in that situation would have added no value, or rather the lack of a meeting would not have reduced the quality of the outcome.

You may be thinking how could someone who has written a book on time management agree to a meeting involving a 500-mile drive and a day of his time without thinking about it? On that I am guilty! I think it also illustrates that there is no better learning than personal experience. The positive lesson I can claim is that I realised my mistake, rectified it and, believe me, I have not made the same mistake since.

Case study 2

I was working with a team of sales people. They were responsible for selling to new customers and maintaining and building existing customer relationships. One of the issues we were discussing was how to get more new customers and look after the existing ones with the current sales resource. The company had introduced a policy, some years previously whereby current customers were visited on a weekly, fortnightly or monthly basis depending on their current business levels or potential for additional business. The current customer visits were taking approximately 50% of a sales person's time. One of the team raised the question, 'why do we visit these current customers on this regular "call cycle" basis?' After much discussion it was obvious that in many cases there were no specific business objectives for these meetings other than a vague notion of customer service. The call cycle had become a routine, accepted by both the sales organisation and the customer. We developed some options. For example, for customers on a fortnightly call cycle, what if this was changed to a visit once per month, with a telephone progress call every two weeks? There were concerns that customers may feel that they were being neglected and that such a change may signal that their business was not being valued. The outcome was an analysis, in conjunction with customers, of how they purchased and what logistics this involved which determined the frequency of meetings needed to fulfil their customer service expectations. The outcome was a more focused approach to routine customer meetings, whereby some would receive more visits, others less, but with regular phone contact to compliment the face-to-face meetings. The result was that the sales people were able to devote more time to new business without reducing service to existing customers.

To me what is to be learned from both of these case studies is our blind acceptance of the need for a meeting. We tend not to question if someone, particularly a customer, calls a meeting. Questioning is not signalling 'I cannot be bothered'. It is about saying 'we are all busy people, therefore is a meeting the most time effective way for us to discuss what we need to achieve?' I stress that meetings are a key part of business life – they are necessary for internal company working, project management, getting new business, building customer relationships, developing teams. However, before committing to a meeting ask the question, 'is this the best use of my time and that of the other person?'

Alternatives to meetings

So what are the alternatives to meetings? In considering them we need to consider two factors. Firstly, which of the options will be most effective in time management terms? For example a telephone call would be more time effective than one of the people involved having to travel a long distance for a face-to-face meeting. While in this book we are focusing on time management time is not the only factor to consider. We also have to answer the question which of the options will provide the best outcome. There is little point in saving time by deciding to organise a telephone conference meeting when in reality it is important that the people meet as there are significant relationship issues that can only be addressed person to person. In fact the result would be wasted time as in this situation a meeting would have to take place anyway. However, this is not always the situation and in many cases there are viable alternatives to a meeting, alternatives that will produce the correct outcome *and* save time.

There is no mystery as to what the options are and I am sure that you are as aware of them as I am:

- a telephone call or conference call where a number of people are involved;
- a letter or an internal memo;
- e-mail;
- a video conference;
- a series of brief one-to-one meetings as they can take less time than assembling a large group.

These are all different ways of communicating in exactly the same way that a meeting is a communication forum. At this stage I am not going to analyse in detail the merits of each. I will cover some of this discussion later, particularly in regard to the use of e-mail, in Chapter 17 on e-world issues. For the moment the purpose in listing the options is to reinforce the fact that these options exist, so that we do not automatically decide on calling a meeting.

There are four key questions you need to ask yourself to help you decide which is the most appropriate communication forum to use.

1. What is my objective – what am I seeking to achieve?

2. To achieve the objective how important is it that the people involved need to meet face to face?

3. Which of the options is going to be most effective in achieving the objective?

4. Which of the options is going to be the most time effective?

You need to use your judgement in making these decisions, and the answers to the four questions will help you make the correct judgement call. This process is also an example of stepping back, investing some time to make time. A three-minute investment of time to decide if a meeting really is necessary will potentially save vast amounts of time for you and your colleagues.

You have made the decision – a meeting is required

So you have decided to call a meeting. This is fine – we have already agreed that meetings are necessary, are often the only viable option you have and can be highly effective. The key word in the last sentence is *can*! A business acquaintance of mine takes the view that a meeting need never take more than 30 minutes if it is well organised. I think that this is an extreme view, and flawed, particularly if you are the one who has to fly to Frankfurt to meet him! However, there are some simple steps that you can take to ensure that a meeting will produce the required outcome and be time effective.

- *Have a goal and an agenda.* Be clear about what you want to achieve and design an agenda that will logically steer the discussion and decision points through to reaching the goal.
- *Give people time.* People need to plan for meetings, possibly prepare a presentation or research information. If they do not have this time there will be missing information which may mean the meeting is delayed or decisions cannot be taken. Of course there is always the crisis meeting where no one has notice. This is reality. However, the majority of meetings can be planned. Remember the rule – plan what you can plan.
- *Impose a time limit.* While I do not subscribe to the '30 minute theory' from my acquaintance from Frankfurt, there is no doubt that a time limit creates focus. Without this we are subject to the law which states that discussion and debate will expand to fill the time available.
- *Someone has to manage the agenda.* It is part of human nature for people to stray off the point, get sidetracked, move the discussion to areas outside the remit of the meeting. Meetings are also a great opportunity for people to further their cause, lobby the participants and make some personal points. This is understandable and to a degree it has to be lived with – but a meeting will not be effective if the participants stray from the goals. Someone has to keep everybody focused and aware of time. In Chapter 12 we discussed behaviour and communication, and analysed the

merits of assertion. Assertion is needed to manage meetings. Be tough on the issues and the time, not on the people!

- *Capture the commitments.* I am sure that you have experienced this – the meeting breaks up, there are vague agreements on what will happen next, but nothing actually does happen! This is because there no definitive agreements and commitments were made. Someone has to capture the commitments and ensure that the action has been logged by those responsible.

- *Summarise at the end.* During the course of, for example, a 45-minute meeting involving five people a lot of ground can be covered. Taking a few minutes at the end of the meeting to summarise what has been discussed, what has been agreed and what commitments have been made will focus people's minds. It reinforces that the meeting has been about action, not just a vague discussion.

- *Confirm and follow up.* The term 'minutes' seems very formal and at odds with the business environment of the twenty-first century, so let us use the term 'meeting report' instead. A brief summary, confirming action points, accountabilities and time scales, will serve as a reminder to the participants and increase the percentage chance of follow-up actions being completed on time. A meeting where there is no outcome, no action, is a total waste of time for all concerned.

Summary

Meetings are expensive in terms of time and money. However, they are an essential element of business life. Technology may have increased the communication options but people still need to meet. However, you should avoid the trap of seeing a meeting as the only form of communication. Consider the options using the checklist in this chapter and make a decision based on which is the best approach in terms of providing the most effective outcomes, and in terms of best use of time for all concerned. If you decide that a meeting is the best option use the guidelines above – following them will ensure that the meeting is focused and will make for most effective use of time.

CHAPTER 16

Think 'team'

Time management and the team

> 'I think this is a great idea, but the rest of the people in my department do not work that way.'

I have lost count of the number of times this comment has been made when I have been facilitating time management workshops. Let me give you the context. We had been discussing, for example, prioritising or how to manage interruptions. The workshop participants were receptive to the new ideas. Their concerns were that because their colleagues or managers did not work in that way, it would be difficult for them to implement the new ideas back at work. This is a totally understandable concern. We have already discussed that we do not work or live in isolation. Other people, how they work, affect us and we affect other people.

Interestingly time management is rarely seen as a topic for team training and development. It is usually seen as personal development, which of course it is, but the team dimension is often missed. You have probably participated in team development workshops in the course of your career. What topics are usually covered? Often creating a shared mission, identifying the barriers to effective team working and developing solutions, agreeing a way of working, evolving a team culture. How individuals in the team manage their time, how this impacts on colleagues or establishing some rules for team time management, in my experience, is rarely on the agenda. Yet it is an important factor, as how others manage their time will impact on you and likewise your time management practices will impact on others. Let me give you an example.

Some time ago I facilitated a number of workshops for a major motor manufacturer. On one workshop the participants were from a number of dealers within the network. Across the participant group the range of functions were represented – sales, service, parts and administration. The discussion groups were lively in that each department was blaming the other departments for wasting their time, dropping unplanned tasks on them with no notice, and demanding unrealistic deadlines. For example, the service department would complain that sales people would suddenly announce that a customer was coming to take delivery of a new car that day. Service would have to carry out the pre-delivery checks, which would mean that some of the scheduled service work on other customers' vehicles could not be completed. The parts department would complain that they were often put under pressure by the service department by suddenly requesting parts that were out of stock. In a busy dealership some crises are inevitable. However, from discussions we found that a significant percentage were avoidable if the individuals thought 'team' when making commitments and demanding action from others. In the first example the sales person knew some time ago that the customer wished to take delivery of the new vehicle on that particular day. The sales person had not planned ahead and informed the service department in good time that they would need to schedule in the pre-delivery check. Even if the customer had suddenly demanded that the delivery day be brought forward, the sales person should not have automatically committed to this without checking if it was possible for the service department.

The conclusions from these discussions were twofold. Firstly, in many cases people were not aware of the impact they were having on others. The sales person was not aware of the current priorities and workload of the service department so genuinely did not realise the impact on them of not planning ahead and giving them sufficient notice. Secondly, many of the issues could be overcome by making straightforward changes to time management practices and thinking at a team level.

Another important point comes out of the above examples. This is that you need to consider teams at two levels. Firstly, there is your immediate team, of which you are a member. Secondly, there are other teams and other departments in the business – in other words, the bigger 'company team'. Within teams and across teams there is a mutual dependency – how you and your team manage your time will impact on others, and how others manage their time will impact you and your team.

Developing your own time management effectiveness in isolation will give you significant benefits. But those benefits will be increased if developing time effectiveness is carried out at a team level. You may be wondering how you can achieve this. If you are a manager or have a team leadership responsibility then it is somewhat easier than if you have no 'direct line authority'. However, the notion of line managers is redundant in many of today's businesses and there is far more opportunity for team members to influence others. But how, in reality, can you influence the time management effectiveness of your colleagues at the same time as developing your own time management practices?

Developing team time management practices

What I suggest you do *not* do is walk into the office stating that you have read a book on time management or have attended a time management course and now you intend to change the way everybody works. I predict that this approach is doomed to failure! My advice is to be selective, decide what changes will have the most effect and work on them. I also recommend you approach the development through suggestion – highlighting mutual benefits will be more effective than telling.

Below I have listed some ideas which I have seen work for others, but I ask you not to just accept this list. Your starting point should be to identify where the major issues are, then decide which of the time management skills we have discussed will be most effective in providing a solution.

- *Identify your frequent contacts.* Identify, say, the 'top five' people, either within or outside your immediate team. The people you frequently work with who are often demanding your time and you their time. Sit down and get a better understanding of their priorities, share your priorities, and identify how you can help each other by changing or modifying time management practices.

- *Suggest some common working practices.* Within your team discuss and decide a set of common working practices. Do not go for an exhaustive list, but identify and implement no more than three things that you have decided among you that will help the team's time management. What these are will be driven by the time management issues you face, but a number of examples that are practical and in my experience work are as follows:

Implement the 'ABC–123' prioritisation system across the team. The effect of everybody prioritising using the same label will make communication a lot easier and will help you to prioritise collectively.

Early morning meeting. A ten-minute get together first thing in the morning is a useful way of establishing the individual and team priorities for the day, identifying who needs time from who and when, what the overall workload looks like, and discussing solutions to any envisaged time issues.

Establish the concept of no interrupt zones. I will be discussing this subject in more detail in Chapter 20. For complex tasks when planning the future, people need time free of interruptions. As a team you can agree when these are and how they are to be managed.

Consider a common system. This may not always be practical if people are already using their own systems, and some people may resent feeling that they are being 'standardised'. However, if the opportunity exists there are many benefits to all team members in using the same time system.

- *Identify the time stolen by other teams.* Within your own team identify the most significant impacts on your time – other teams and departments making demands on your time with non-scheduled requests. Set up meetings to discuss the issues and their impact and identify solutions by agreeing a change in time management practice.

- *Identify where you steal time from other teams.* Other teams will be more receptive to your suggestions that they change their time management practices if you make it a two-way process. You ask them where they feel you impact on their time unnecessarily and try to provide a solution.

- *Develop a language.* Now, you may think that this sounds gimmicky, but developing a language code in the team can genuinely help. For example, a colleague approaches you. They want your input on an unscheduled task. You are under pressure to complete an important and urgent task. It is much easier to say 'A1, can I call you in 30 minutes' than go into an explanation of what you are doing and why it is difficult for you to stop what you are doing now. A manager in one company I worked in had a notice that he put on his desk when he needed interrupt-free time. It said simply, 'No'. That may seem rather direct and not supportive of cooperative team working. In fact it was fine, as it was part of the team language.

Summary

- The first step is to develop your own time effectiveness – this is personal development.

- Do not stop there. Introduce some time management practices to your colleagues and agree some team time management practices.

- Discuss 'time stealers' with other teams you work with and arrive at solutions.

- If you are involved in organising or contributing to a team development programme, introduce the notion that effective time management is a key ingredient of team working.

CHAPTER 17

The e-world issues

The e-world and time management

The subject of the e world, the implications for all of us, in life and work terms would fill a book in itself. We believe that we have seen the revolution, but in reality we are only just seeing the start of it. The advent of the e-world is driven by the Internet and the possibilities it gives us for how we lead our lives, in every sense – how it can free us from the daily drudgery of travelling to the office and from the chore of the weekly shop, how it changes the way in which we learn and receive information, how we handle and process our family finances. The list is endless.

While technology has been the driver in the context of time management, we need to look at the other changes that have taken place in recent years – the dismantling of formal business structures, the move to matrix and project-based organisations, the shift from employment to short-term contracts, the advent of virtual teams. Here I am using the term 'e-world' to describe in total terms the new culture and environment, not just the technological aspects.

The debate about the implications of these changes for all of us goes on. Quoting numbers about how many people are on line and the amount of time the average person spends on the Internet each day is a pointless exercise – by the time I have finished this chapter the statistics will have moved on. Undoubtedly the implications are far reaching, from how it will effect society and our infrastructure to the possible effects on future generations who become insular from spending too much time on the lone pursuit of surfing the Internet rather than being engaged in 'real' human interaction. However, I must practise what I am preaching, and stay focused on the subject of time management, and the implications of the e-world on how we manage our time.

The possibilities for us to improve our time effectiveness by intelligent use of technology are vast and exciting. It potentially gives us freedom to plan our time more flexibly to fit in with our individual schedules. We can order a book at any time rather than between the hours of 9.00 a.m. and 5.30 p.m. when the local bookshop is open. We can book a holiday on a Saturday evening, not having to visit a travel agent. We can send messages to work colleagues from our homes without the need to go to the office. We can collect important messages from our mobile phones while sitting in the car. We can conduct an interactive e-mail conversation. It is amazing, when compared with the communication tools available just a few years ago.

However, as with most things in life, there is a downside, a potential negative. In the context of the e-world and the implications for our time management, there are four key issues that we need to address. If we do not, the potential benefits become threats, taking time rather than not saving it. These four key issues are as follows:

- *E-mail.* The facility that is available to all of us, the facility that potentially can make us so much more effective, can become a time thief.

- *The pace and the urgency.* The tendency, with the advent of electronic communication, is that the expectations of the speed of response have risen dramatically. This expectation has implications for people's abilities to manage these pressures.

- *The growth of remote home-based working.* There are potentially massive benefits for people in terms of the freedom it gives, but there are also significant risks in terms of how people manage their time in work and life terms.

- *The replacement of formal structures of people in a central base with virtual geographically dispersed teams.* The notion of working in a number of remote project teams is fascinating, but again there are implications.

We will look at each of these in turn, identify the potential time management issues, and provide some solutions.

E-mail

The subject of e-mail divides opinion. There are the e-mail junkies who measure their productivity by how many e-mails they have sent and received during a working day; they have given up all other forms of communication, sending e-mails to people sitting a few desks away. At the other extreme there are those who see e-mail as a high technology version of the in-tray which grows ever larger, representing a burden that must be cleared. Even these people can take a private pleasure in declaring how big their 'in-box' is, as if the number of e-mails received in a day is in direct proportion to status and power!

In my opinion there is no doubt that e-mail is an incredibly powerful tool in helping us to be more effective time managers. Applying some simple rules to prevent the misuse of e-mail will ensure that it is a contributor to managing time rather than a detractor.

Action e-mails in the same way as you would a paper in-tray

It is honesty time again. Are you a compulsive e-mail checker? Those working from a home base with a dial-up modem suffer from this least, as it is a deliberate action to dial up a connection. Those who have access via a network are the real sufferers. They know from looking at the screen that there are new arrivals in the inbox. They may be working in a totally different application when the screen flashes up the new arrivals, stating who they are from and what the topic is. The compulsion is to stop what you are doing, read the new mails and action them. If you are a compulsive checker have you ever thought about how many times during a day you access the inbox? Have you ever thought about how long it takes? Not just the checking, but the diversion created by opening up the e-mails, the time lost on the task you were working on, and the time to refocus back on the original task. Over a week the lost time is significant.

Let us go back in time, to the 'pre' e-world. How did people generally action their post? Well, they would open the post in the morning, decide which items must be actioned that day, which were for action later, which items were for information and which items could be immediately filed. This done, people got on with their day and the next time they would action their post would be the next morning. You see, the post was not arriving throughout the day, so there was no compulsion or pressure to keep opening it. I appreciate that this is not a direct analogy as the e-mail traffic is replacing some telephone calls that would have been received in the pre e-world. However, if the sender requires immediate action they would, or should, pick up the phone as opposed to send an e-mail. More of that later.

What are the learning points? What can you do minimise the distractions caused by e-mail traffic? Here are some suggestions:

- Think of e-mail as the equivalent of the daily post and the in-tray.

- Check e-mails each morning and allocate the priorities to each.

- As part of your daily plan allocate specific times throughout the day – for example, lunchtime and mid-afternoon – to check for new e-mails, and again prioritise accordingly.

- Make it part of your routine to check last thing before you leave work, as actioning new e-mails will become part of your day plan for tomorrow.

There is nothing complex or sophisticated about these guidelines! It is about building the task into your daily plan, and being disciplined. Avoid the distraction caused by compulsive checking. Of course, there are always exceptions to the rule. There will be the e-mail you are expecting containing important information which you know will require urgent action. You will look out for it, and given the prioritisation guidelines we have already discussed, you will see it as a high priority task that overrides your planned schedule. But do not get sidetracked into opening all of your e-mails, just to see what they are about, at the same time. They can wait!

Do not circulate to the world

I am sure that you know about the other e-mail syndrome. This is the 'who may have a remote interest in this e-mail, and if I think they have I will copy them'. The result is that some e-mails are copied to a cast of thousands. If you analyse the e-mails that you receive some are directly for you for you to action and some are for your information and are relevant, while others are irrelevant and take up your time needlessly. The problem is that it is so easy to transmit e-mails to a large number of people. Pre e-world, when memos or letters were sent, this required effort, so there was an in-built check of who really needed to know about this. You can help other people save their time by being considered about who you send and copy e-mails to. By thinking 'team', as discussed in Chapter 16, agree with your colleagues a 'protocol' for e-mail circulation, set a rule that says e-mail copies are restricted to those who really need to know. The objective is to save your time, and the time of your colleagues.

Ask yourself if an e-mail is best

E-mails are quick, easy and effective. There is no doubt about this. For these reasons some people have fallen into the trap of using e-mail for all communications without thinking about the alternatives. The other motive for this, which may be subconscious, is the high-tech equivalent of abdication. Sending a mail takes the action off your desk and puts it on someone else's. Again, let us be honest – in these situations it is easier to send the-mail than have a conversation and risk a conflict!

How many e-mail communications require a follow-on phone call to agree an action, get an answer, discuss an issue? I believe that the answer is 'most'. So why not pick up the telephone to start with, talk to the person to discuss what needs to be discussed and agree what needs to be agreed? I have stressed throughout that I am not trying to impose rules but provide guidelines. And guidelines require you to exercise judgement. For example, it is perfectly legitimate to e-mail somebody to provide them with information that they will require before they can have a meaningful telephone conversation with you. In such a situation this will save time, as trying to relay the background information over the telephone will take longer than sending a mail. The e-mail adds value in the communication process. The key is to ask yourself the question 'will sending an e-mail add value, and save time, or is it more time effective to make a telephone call in the first place?' If the answer comes back no, the e-mail does not add value, then do not press the send button. Pick up the phone instead.

We have discussed e-mail versus making a telephone call. I would like to end on what is, I hope, an obvious point. That is, if you are in the same office as the person you are about to mail to, possibly a few desks away, think not of the telephone option, but of walking over to see them. Much has been written on the possible implications of e-mail on team relationships because people are interacting less. This is a serious point, but in pure time management terms alone there can be a negative effect. A face-to-face dialogue is usually more effective in resolving an issue, achieving a common understanding of a complex problem or reaching a decision than a string of e-mails. Again, judgement is called for. E-mail will be the most effective way of communicating a vast range of data to colleagues, even if they are next to you, *if* the e-mail completes that communication. If, however, it does not and some other dialogue is needed then forget the e-mail, go and see the person instead. They may say that they are working on an 'A1'. Can they wander over to see you in an hour? Surely this is positive? You now understand their time pressures. You have the opportunity to flag that your 'interrupt' really is a priority, requiring urgent attention – if indeed it does. This is preferable to an e-mail war!

The pace and urgency in the e-world

The pace of business and life in the twenty-first century is frantic. The trend, started in the 1980s and 1990s, is set to continue. There are a number of drivers. The removal of national barriers has led to the globalisation of markets. Technological advances mean that product life cycles have repeatedly decreased. Increased consumer awareness leads to increased expectations of service. Changes that would take five years in the old economy now take as many months. Competition is fierce – companies that were once dominant locally find themselves losing their independence in the international environment. The advances in information technology have resulted in more rapid communication – people now expect a response to a request in hours not days. In the old economy, companies worked to five-year strategic plans. Now a total market situation can change in a few months. And during the same period organisations have cut out layers of management and reduced overheads to increase their competitiveness.

It is exciting, it is dynamic, it is challenging. But it creates problems in terms of how we manage our time, our ability to be effective. The human being has not evolved at the same pace. Yes, we have better training and more technological resources, but fundamentally we are the same people, with the same number of hours available, but with more and more varied things to do. It is an issue, a very real problem. In recent years we have witnessed the birth of stress-related illness, the result of ever increasing pressures of work caused by the factors described above.

But is there a solution? You will recall that in my introduction I stated that there was no single answer for managing time more effectively. Making inroads into taming time is a result of making changes and developing skills in a number of areas. Overlaying this statement with the pace and rate of change that we have to manage in the e-world highlights the time management strategies that we need to take. In highlighting these points I will introduce some additional 'mindset items' as well as reinforce some of the skills that I have already introduced. Here are my suggestions, my guidelines. Remember that there is no fixed formula.

- *Learn to live with uncertainty*. This is not a statement of defeat, it is an acknowledgement of reality. Some people are inherently more comfortable with the unknown than others. We all know people who thrive on change and uncertainty, while others, who have carefully formulated plans, feel uncomfortable when their planning assumptions are overturned. It is unlikely that the pace and rate of change we are experiencing will slow down – in fact the opposite is probably true. In a strong gale it is the fixed rigid structure that is destroyed. Which leads me on to my second point.

- *Balance focus and flexibility*. Living in a fast-changing world does not mean that we can forget the need to be focused on goals. I have previously made the point that the greater the level of dynamics and unplanned tasks, the greater the need for planning. Being focused on short-, medium- and long-term goals is still relevant in a fast-moving, ever changing environment. What you must do is revisit those goals more frequently to check that they are still valid. If they are not, be prepared to change them. This does not mean that you change them without question. If they are still valid, hold on to them, defend them. Which leads me on to my third point.

- *Even if the goals are still valid, be prepared to change the route.* You will recall my earlier analogy of your goals being the destination and your tasks the milestones along the way. In a dynamic world, even if your goals remain valid you may have to modify the route you are taking to get there. The non-planned may take priority over the planned. Which takes me to point four.

- *Prioritise the priorities.* The demands in the e-world may be greater, there are more things to do, and the priorities change more rapidly. However, you still have only so many hours. Yes, there may be times when you are prepared to put in more hours, but unless you are prepared to continually commit more time unconditionally, you have to make decisions. This involves prioritising the priorities, so that you are focused on the most important actions.

- *Assert and question.* The e-world may be dynamic and fast-changing. This does not mean that change is always right, or that priorities should always be changing. Change is not always a given – it can, and should, be questioned. Given the pace of change and the consequent pressures there is the risk of a knee-jerk reaction, the instant change of direction. This can be expensive in time terms, so it should be questioned.

In summary, in Chapter 10, 'Why plan if it will all change anyway', I introduced the principle that the more chaotic and fast-moving the environment the greater the need for planning and organisation. This is particularly true in the e-world, where the conditions are such that focus and flexibility must be balanced.

The growth of home-based working

The last few years have seen a big increase in the number of people working from home. All of the forecasts predict that the number of home-based workers will continue to grow. There have been two principal contributors to this trend.

Firstly, employees of large companies can now work away from the office at least part of the time as technology enables easy and cost-effective remote access to a company's systems and therefore information. There is no need to be in an office to fulfil at least some of the tasks. A number of companies have been able to implement a 'hot desk' policy, whereby, during visits to the office, the remote workers have the use of a workstation.

The second driver is the growth in the number of the self-employed. For many people short-term contracts have replaced fixed contracts of employment. People are employed on a project basis, and often are working with more than one company at the same time.

This revolution in how people work has generated a lot of debate. There are concerns about the loss of social contact that home workers will experience as it is acknowledged that the workplace is also a social place. How will people cope with working in isolation for at least some of the time? We need to put the wider debate to one side and focus on the implications on how we manage our time.

I know a number of people – I am sure you do – who have stopped travelling to an office and now work predominantly from home. I have spoken to people who spent up to three hours a day on the round trip commuting daily to London, while others spent up to four hours a day in a car simply to get to the office and back. When they were doing it was a part of the working day, part of an established routine, not enjoyable, but accepted. Suddenly, with the switch to working from home there are three to four hours additional time, unproductive time freed up; time that can be used effectively. What an opportunity! You have the freedom of working in your own environment, and you can take the opportunity to spend more time with your family, create a better work–life balance and work when it suits you. This is all true – it is a time management opportunity. Someone who lives close to me spent many years working in London, catching the 7.00 a.m. train, and returning home usually 13 hours later. He changed his job and became a home-based contract worker. I now see him walking his dogs at 7.30 most mornings, relaxed in casual clothes, before going back home to his office to start the working day. This has to be better than standing on the 7.00 a.m. to London

So has technology enabled us to find paradise, to discover the ideal working environment with more time to achieve our goals? I repeat – it is a real opportunity! However, opportunities need to be realised, the benefits are not automatic. A number of home-based workers have told me that they find that they are in fact working longer hours than before. Some acknowledge that while the work intensity may have reduced they are often working well into the evening. Many have found it hard to 'close the office door' and walk away because the office is always no more than a few feet away. Others have found that having escaped the distractions in an office environment other distractions have replaced them – for example, being co-opted for the school run mid-afternoon when they have an important report to finish. As the home is now the office the potential problems can be closely related to personal circumstances. People with a young family have more factors to balance, particularly in the school holidays, than someone living on their own. People with the luxury of an office away from the house – for example, a garden house or a converted outbuilding – find it easier to close the office door than people who use a converted bedroom as an office.

It is different being a home-based worker. You may be free of a number of the issues faced by office-based workers, but you will inherit others. The guidelines below are designed to highlight the issues and to provide some practical advice on how to address them. Not everyone will experience the same issues so focus on the ones that are relevant to you. Most of the points are equally applicable to home-based employees and the self-employed, though some have a greater relevance for the self-employed, and this is highlighted in the text.

- *Discipline.* I have already said that this as a prerequisite for effective time management. We may blame others for stealing our time, but we are also our own time stealers. Imposing your own discipline in a traditional environment within an imposed office structure was important. Given a home-working environment, with little or no external control, it is doubly important.

- *Regard your partner and family as the rest of the team.* Let me explain what I mean by this. In Chapter 16, 'Think "team"', we discussed the need to formulate a code of practice for time management with your colleagues. If you are working at home, in a sense your partner and family become your colleagues. You need to discuss and agree a framework, in a sense a set of rules for how you intend to integrate an office and a home under one roof.

- *Retain what worked for you at the office.* Switching from an office to a home-based environment need not be revolution. What worked for you before should be retained. This can be a number of things from the obvious to the not so obvious. For example, a client told me of one of their staff who had become a home worker who continued to dress formally each morning even though he was not setting foot outside of his home. He was used to wearing a suit, it signalled work, and he found that retaining the habit helped him stay disciplined and focused. For me one of the benefits of working from home is being able to dress casually; even when office based we have had a relaxed dress code, from the day we opened our UK office back in 1989, long before 'dress down' came into fashion. However, this is about personal preference and what works for you. If wearing a suit when working from home helps, then wear one!

- *Remember the rules of time management.* Everything we have discussed so far, and all of the points we have yet to cover, are equally relevant for people working in a home environment as for those who are office based. This may sound obvious, but sometimes the change of environment can cause us to forget the core principles and skills.

- *Maximise the energy curve opportunity.* We have already discussed tackling the complex, taxing tasks in your high energy periods. Given the freedom you have when working from home you have the opportunity to capitalise on this. Freed from travel time and the other constraints of conventional working, you could, for example, if you are an early energy person, be working at 5.00 a.m. (particularly in the summer with early light) and have finished your working day by the early afternoon.

- *Think seven not five days.* No, I am not suggesting that you now work seven days a week! I think that this point is more applicable to self-employed people running their own businesses. In the context of creating a healthy work–life balance you now have seven days to plan to create the balance. For example, it may be more convenient to take a leisure day mid-week and work on a Saturday. I appreciate that there are still parameters you have to work within; for example, you may have to attend client meetings, which would not take place at weekends. However, you genuinely have the opportunity to think outside the box of the conventional working week. Many people who are self-employed and have this freedom still prefer to compartmentalise the week as work and the weekends as leisure. This is understandable, but the principle remains – outside of a conventional office environment you have the opportunity to balance your work and out of work time more evenly.

- *Remember the extra tasks you need to build into your time schedule.* This point is specifically for people who have moved from employee status to that of contractor or consultant working on short-term contract possibly for more than one company. You will have lost the 'life support systems' available to employees in large corporations. The photocopier always worked, the stationery cupboard was always full, insurance and tax issues were all handled by someone else. As a self-employed home-worker they land on your desk. You will need to allocate time to these 'maintenance tasks'. You will also have additional 'future' tasks – maintaining and developing a network of business contacts, identifying future business, etc. You need to identify what these tasks are and build them in to your time plan.

- *Lock the office door.* This is about discipline, and specifically about ensuring that you do not suffer from the 'working day drift' – this is avoiding opening the office, the room next door, to complete few more jobs, after 'office hours'. It is tempting, there are times when it will be necessary, but set some clear rules and keep to them. A few years ago I was working with a Canadian training consultant on a potential project. I have never known anybody who was so prompt at responding to e-mails. I calculated that he must have been at his PC in the middle of the night, his time, to respond in the timescales he did. When we eventually met he admitted that he was a poor sleeper so would often get up to make a drink in the middle of the night. On his way downstairs to the kitchen he could not resist stopping off at his office to check the inbox for new messages, and reply to them immediately. He had not learned to lock the office door!

In summary, being a home-based worker provides real opportunities to make most effective use of your time. You are freed from travel time to the office and back, and you have more freedom in terms of how you plan your work. However, there are some potential risks. Remember to apply the time management skills we have discussed in a home-work environment in the same way that an office-based person would. Highlight which of the above eight points apply to you if you are a home-based worker, and decide which ideas and principles you are going to take on board and implement.

The replacement of fixed centrally based structures with temporary remote teams

In the old world economy there were a number of givens – there was, in relative terms, a high degree of predictability. There were formal organisation structures, there were established career paths. Job roles were established and well defined.

Although the features of the old economy have not totally disappeared, there has been a shift. More people are working in project teams. More people are working in virtual teams. More people are working on a fixed-term contract basis. Job roles are more fluid. Companies are merging or developing strategic partnerships. There is a lower level of stability. Life is less predictable.

What are the time management implications for people working in this new environment? The following sections outline what I believe are some of the key implications, and provide some suggestions as to how they can be addressed.

The 'plannables' are less fixed

In a fixed job role the actions that can be planned are reasonably consistent. In a project-based role the parameters change from project to project. Therefore, reviewing the planned actions, both 'now' and 'future' tasks, will need to be carried out more frequently.

Relationships keep changing

In a formal office based structure there is a relatively high level of consistency. If you are working with a number of virtual, fluid teams there are more and different relationships to manage. We have said that time management requires a team approach, an agreed set of rules which everybody buys into. This process, agreeing a way of working, has to be established every time a new project team is set up. This means an initial investment of time, so we return to the principle that you need to invest time to make time.

Organisations and resources are less clear

In a fluid organisation identifying the resources available, where the centres of knowledge are, where the potential support is, is less clear. One of the key skills in these organisations is that of networking – setting up your own network of contacts you can call on for advice and help when needed. Investing time in networking will help you secure resources when you need them, identify where specific actions can be delegated and give you access to the knowledge bank that is available. I cannot stress enough how important this is. In the old-style businesses the organisation charts told you this. In the new-style businesses you have to find it out for yourself! Again, it requires an investment of time, but the resources a network will provide you with will help your time management in the mid and long term.

There are higher levels of chaos

This is driven not just by the dismantling of formal structures but by the overall pace of business. The danger is that we become more task driven, more focused on the short term. I believe that the answer is to keep stepping back. I have established this as a key principle of effective time management in any role or situation, but it is even more important in this environment. This is related to, but has a different context from, the point relating to the 'plannables' being less fixed. That was concerned about reviewing actions more frequently. This is about stepping back to ensure you retain the correct perspective, and that you are still clear about the destination.

Summary

In summary, the e-world provides us with the opportunities to develop our time effectiveness through the flexibility and technology that it provides. To realise these opportunities may involve some changes in work practices to enable you adapt to the new environment. The key challenges are to use technology intelligently, to manage to live with uncertainty, to balance focus and flexibility, to adapt to working remotely, and to learn to work effectively in less formal structures.

I would like to end on the key message that all of the time management skills we have discussed are even more critical in the e-world than in the old economy: the greater the rate of change, the greater the need to be planned and organised.

CHAPTER 18

Be decisive – go for the hard tasks

We all have these tasks sitting on our desks. The ones we do not really want to do but know we must. Who has not thought of reasons to delay starting them, by talking ourselves into the belief that another task, something that we feel more comfortable doing, has a greater priority. Once we have rationalised this to ourselves we put the hard task back onto the for 'action list' to be looked at again tomorrow. If this is something you do not suffer from you can move on from this chapter. If you believe that you do put off tackling the hard tasks then read on!

We are all human, so in certain situations this behaviour is understandable. We may find the task boring; we may find it daunting; at the extreme we may even doubt our ability to complete it. However, if it is a legitimate task we have to address it. By legitimate I mean:

- it is a task that contributes to the achievement of your goals;
- it is therefore part of your job role;
- it is not a task that should or could be delegated.

This is not restricted to work. There are tasks in our private lives that we put off because we do not want to do them, or they may involve acknowledging an issue a problem.

This is called procrastination – being indecisive. You may argue that by ignoring the hard task you have made a decision – to ignore it. In reality this is not true, as you have in effect postponed the decision that you know you have to make. The non-technical term is 'burying your head in the sand'!

How does this procrastination impact your time management? There are three major effects. Firstly the indecision, the process of rationalising why you should put the task off, does, in itself, take time. This is time that you could be using productively. Secondly, you are not working to your priorities if the hard task you are putting to one side has an important label attached to it. Finally, you will create a crisis for yourself, as eventually you will have to face up the fact that it must be completed. By this time there is an urgent as well important label attached to it.

There are six suggestions below intended to help you overcome the problem. Simply by implementing one of these may provide the solution, or a combination may be needed.

- *Acknowledge that it is there.* As I have already said, putting the task off is not the answer. Acknowledge that it is there. That is the starting point.

- *Prioritise on a rational basis.* Make your decisions on priorities in relation to contribution to your objectives, not on what you prefer to be working on.

- *A complex task can be daunting.* If it is, break it down into its constituent parts. In time management terms this is called 'eating elephants'. The technique is to break the task down into a series of smaller tasks which approached in this way are easier to manage. It is rather like treating a large task as a mini project. Another analogy is to think of the goal as the destination and completing a task takes you along the road to that destination. Think of breaking the task down as completing, for example, five runs of five miles rather than trying to attempt a marathon.

- *Choose a high energy period to tackle these tasks.* This will give you the best chance of succeeding and making inroads.

- *Admit your doubts.* If you are genuinely concerned about your ability, be that because of a skill or a knowledge gap, then admit it, firstly to yourself, and then to a colleague or your boss. Saying that you cannot do something is not a sign of weakness; it is a sign of confidence. It will save you a lot of time in wasted effort.

- *Regard the challenge of tackling a hard task as a motivation, not a burden.* Think forward to the feeling of satisfaction you will experience when you have achieved it.

I believe that we can think ourselves into believing 'this will be difficult'. Of course, once we have convinced ourselves of this it *will* be difficult. Often it is the perception that is the problem and not the reality. In my experience, there is a rule that says the more difficult I think the task will be, the easier the reality of completing it is. The reverse is also true! We approach some tasks with confidence and a feeling of 'I can do this without thinking about it' to discover that it becomes a source of stress, tension and problems.

In summary, do not put off the decisions about the hard tasks. If they are important, they will not go away, so schedule to do them in a high energy period. We can think ourselves into the issue. Follow the guidelines above. They will help you to be decisive, to tackle the hard issues and to prevent wasted time.

CHAPTER 19

Task batching

With the click of a mouse a personal computer can switch, at [an] instant, from one type of task to another. One second it can [be] producing a report, seconds later it can be in a spreadsheet application, sending an e-mail, producing a presentation, [or] connecting to your favourite website.

The human brain is, in my view, undoubtedly superior, [in] ultimate terms, to the capability of a personal computer. However, in its ability to switch seamlessly from one task to another, with[out] loss in productivity, the personal computer has most of us beat[en]. The human brain is generally more effective when working on [one] task, or type of task, and completing it before moving on [to] something different. There is no standard human being. So[me] people are able to switch tasks more comfortably than others. [It is] a commonly held view that women are more comfortable at mu[lti]tasking than men. So different people have different abilities task switching than others, but the general statement – people are less effective when switching tasks than when completing one task before moving on to the next – holds true.

I know that, if I am mid-way through writing a letter or producing a client visit report then divert to make two phone calls or to have a brief meeting with a colleague before returning to the letter or report, this is not the most effective way of working. My total time to complete that client visit report, if I start and complete it in one uninterrupted session, is significantly less than if I start it, leave it and then come back to it. This is because every time I task switch I go through a brief acclimatisation period, as my brain adjusts from one task to the next.

I am sure that you will have experienced the same feeling. You leave the report half way through, and when you come back to it you have to recall what point you were at and you may have to read through the last few paragraphs to tune your mind back into the content and the context. This takes time.

To task switch once, then go back to the original task, probably takes little time. But how many times during a day or a week are we task switching before we have completed the first task? Each time we do this we are impacting on our effectiveness, therefore wasting time. On a bad day, full of crises, when you are being driven into ongoing task switching, you probably at some stage sit back and say to yourself 'I just cannot think straight.'

Can you relate to this? The problem is that your brain is getting confused with all of the switching demands being put upon it. At the extreme you end up not being able to complete any of the tasks effectively. In Part 4, 'Staying focused', we discussed ways in which you can manage these sidetracks and diversions.

To develop this theme, if we batch tasks of the same type, and plan to complete them as a block, we become even more effective than when we a complete a task and move onto another, different type of task. This is because our brain tunes into the particular type of task, and as we move on to the second and third task of the same batch we become quicker, more effective. We are completing each one in less time. We are saving time. Returning to my previous example, I know that if I have to complete five client visit reports and allocate time to complete them as a batch I am working most productively. They get easier, I am tuned into that type of task, my brain is not having to significantly reacclimatise as I complete one and move on to the next.

There are two key learning points so far. You will be more productive if you complete one task before moving on to the next. You will be even more productive if you plan to work on a series of tasks of the same type *en bloc*. Of course, in the real world the unplanned will happen, and sometimes the priorities dictate that you have to move from one task type to another. This is inevitable. Let us go back to one the principles we have already discussed – plan what is plannable. When mapping out your daily plans batch tasks of the same type wherever possible. Some task types will be more complex, more demanding than others. Allocate the demanding task types for your high energy times and the more routine ones to your lower energy periods.

The major opportunities for task batching are probably in the 'now' tasks. The 'future' tasks will probably be more specific and possibly project based. The most common task types which are relevant to most functions are as follows.

- *Making telephone calls.* If as part of your daily task list there are a number of telephone calls to be made, plan to do them *en bloc*. Some of the most successful sales people I have met allocate time to blocks of calls to new prospects. These are hard calls as often the rejection rate is high. They find that they become more effective, in terms of success and time, as they get into the session.

- *Writing reports and letters.* This relates back to my earlier example. The structure of one report may be similar to the next one. So the only acclimatisation the brain has to make is the switch of subject, not how to approach and structure it. This will save time.

- *Sending and receiving e-mail.* This is an overlap with writing reports and letters, but I have given e-mail its own category. We have discussed its significance in Chapter 17, 'The e-world issues'. Allocate time to sending, receiving and prioritising the additions to the inbox as a single task type. This will help you to avoid the trap of dipping into the e-mail system throughout the day and impacting on the time allocated to other tasks.

- *Numeric tasks.* Your job may involve analysing cash flow projections, activity reports, marketing campaign response statistics. These type of tasks use a different part of the brain than that used for writing a report. If there are a number of tasks of this nature within your job role look at the possibilities to batch them.

- *Maintenance tasks.* Most jobs have a number of routine tasks that may not be that significant but nonetheless must be completed. Allocate time to these in a relatively low energy period.

Before moving on think of the main tasks that you have to complete, and consider the possibilities of categorising them into different task types. Then look at the practicalities of completing them in batches. It will not always be possible for other reasons, but test this approach where you can, and see if it saves you time. Finally, I am not suggesting that you devote an entire day to one task type. Change and variety is also necessary!

CHAPTER 20

'No interrupt' zones

In previous chapters we have discussed:

- the impact of unscheduled tasks and interruptions on our time management;

- the fact that some unscheduled tasks and interruptions are valid in that they represent a higher priority than the task that you are working on;

- how to manage these potential sidetracks by using assertive behaviour, so that you can hold onto your priorities – this may involve you in negotiating deadlines;

- how viewing time management as a team activity will help establish some agreed time management rules across the team to help everybody.

Creating 'no interrupt' zones is a time management action that links in to all of the above points. What do I mean by 'no interrupt' zones? These are specific windows of time in a working day where your *plan* is to be free of interruptions so that you can focus on a specific task most effectively. In the previous chapter we discussed task batching and the fact that people work most effectively if they complete one task at a time or tasks that are similar. If you can successfully set up interrupt free zones then you will save time and achieve more.

The cynics are probably now thinking that this is fine in theory but will never work in the real world! I am not pretending that this is easy, and the practicality of it will be influenced by the type of job that you have. For example, people in very event-driven, reactive roles may find it more difficult than people whose role is more focused to planning and the longer term. However, I believe it is possible for all of us to set up these free zones if we approach it in the right way.

Approaching the task by taking the following steps will help.

- *Step 1.* Look at your working day or week and decide which time windows offer the best opportunities for you to set up an 'interrupt free' zone. In most jobs there is a reasonably constant pattern of peaks and troughs in terms of unplanned tasks hitting you. For example, if you receive a number of phone calls early morning or last thing in the afternoon your chance of setting up your free zone then would be remote. If you are a manager or a team leader it could be that your team needs a relatively high access to you during the first hour of the day.

- *Step 2.* Identify which of your tasks require the most concentrated blocks of time for you to complete them most effectively. Of course the simple answer is that you would be more effective at completing all of your tasks if you had no interruptions! You will have to prioritise. Generally planning tasks, formulating medium- and long-term goals and complex project work benefit most from non interrupted time.

- *Step 3.* Decide what window of time you can practically set aside. The luxury of three days no interrupt time would be paradise, but not practical for most of us. A half day is probably the most at a practical level, with two hours being more representative. You may not need the facility every day, but feel that two zones a week would be all that is needed.

- *Step 4.* Introduce the idea to your immediate team and colleagues from other departments with whom you have regular contact. Suggest that you all set up interrupt free zones – yes it is a two-way street! You cannot request the facility for yourself and not be prepared to agree to it for others. However, there must be a balance. There is no benefit in everybody setting up their zones unless there is going to be a time benefit, so there has to be an openness about why you feel you need it, for what tasks and what the benefits will be. There has to be cooperation and commitment from team and colleagues for this to work.

- *Step 5*. Agree what the no interrupt time windows are to be, and also what priority interrupts will be allowed.
- *Step 6*. Review progress after one month. Establish what is working and what is not and fine tune as necessary.

As with all plans this will not work all of the time. Some of your planned no interrupt times will get completely overturned. That is reality, it is bound to happen. I have said a number of times before that the non-planned may take a priority. This does not invalidate the principle.

Described as a six-step process this all sounds very mechanistic, and in a sense any planning is. However, there are two other key factors. Firstly, I will return to the term 'mindset item'. Establishing these zones as part of the way you work will require a change of thinking for some people. We are conditioned to interruptions. Most people are willing to help and will drop what they are doing to help a colleague. Sometimes we even welcome the interruption. It can take your discipline – yours and others – to make it work. Secondly, this is not something that you can implement on your own. It is a team item. Here I mean team in the broadest sense of the word, as you need to involve colleagues from other functions. Identify the people who you demand time of on a regular basis, and the people who are frequently requesting your time. Pilot the idea with this initial small network, assess the benefits and then suggest it to others.

In summary, setting up no interrupt zones and being disciplined will provide you with time management benefits. Do not get frustrated if sometimes they do not work – the principle is sound. Work with your colleagues on this, as it also requires their understanding and agreement.

CHAPTER 21

Realistic time estimation

Other people and unexpected events impact on our time and cause us pressure. We also cause our own time pressures. I have already made this point in relation to handling interruptions and a tendency in many of us to accept any interruption regardless of its importance or relevance. We cause our own time pressures in another way – by over-committing to deadlines.

A manager who once worked for me was a master at this. Let me paint you a picture. Can we have some more honesty time? As the story unfolds ask yourself if you show some of these characteristics.

He was highly committed – first to arrive in the morning, last to leave at night. He was running a busy sales department so he genuinely had a heavy schedule to manage. However, he was making his life more difficult than it needed to be. He took a number of phone calls each day, mainly from customers and other departments requesting information. His typical answer was 'give me 15 minutes and I will get straight back to you.' Throughout the day numerous people would be in and out of his office, making requests for his time, asking for information. His usual answer was 'I will get the answer back to you within the hour.' He was perpetually manoeuvring himself into a corner, a corner consisting of too many commitments and not enough time. He was writing cheques that his credit, in terms of time, he could not honour!

Nobody could fault his commitment and willingness – but he was an appalling time manager. Not surprisingly he was working in chaos. We discussed his habit of over-committing. His response was twofold. He had many phone calls and people visiting his office. He was always being asked to drop what he was doing and involve himself in some other task. This is an issue of managing interruptions, which we have already discussed. The second part of his response was that everybody always wants everything yesterday, what could he do? There is an issue here of negotiating deadlines, which we have also covered. However, the key issue, in terms of over-committing, is that he was setting the deadlines himself, by making commitments to get back to someone in 15 minutes or providing an answer within the hour. In many cases the requester was not making the deadline – he was. The person he promised to get back to within 15 minutes would probably been happy with an answer by the end of the day. The person he committed to get information to within the hour could well have lived with an answer by tomorrow morning. He was falling into the trap of:

- committing to a deadline without considering how long the task would take to complete;
- not asking the person making the request what an acceptable response time would be;
- taking on additional work without thinking about the impact on his ability to complete the existing workload on his desk;
- reacting to the latest demand without recognising the need to prioritise on what is important;
- making the assumption that the person making the request *had* to have the information in the next 15 minutes.

His motives were honourable – commit to everybody that he would give their request the highest priority. He was trying to be helpful. In fact he was being unhelpful. He was over-committing and under-performing. He was raising expectations and failing. People did not get the answers when they thought they would, so they would phone him to check what had happened. This took time. He spent considerable time phoning people pleading for an extension to the over-ambitious deadline that he had set himself. This also took time. He was building himself a workload and set of deadlines that he could not possibly achieve.

As when covering negotiating deadlines and managing interruptions in Part 4 I would like to state the need for balance. If you receive a request, and you can commit the next 15 minutes to actioning it without impacting on your ability to meet your current commitments then fine – do it. I am not recommending an approach that is always pushing out the deadline as far as possible. This will be seen as unhelpful, and you will be viewed as being non-cooperative, as not being a team player.

So what are the guidelines for becoming a realistic time estimator, for avoiding the trap of over-committing and under-performing? Consider the following:

- Keep in the forefront of your mind the thought that things generally take longer than you thought they would.

- Do not make a rash commitment to action a task for someone without considering how long it will take, the possibility that you may need the help of a colleague to complete the task (they may not be available) and what your overall workload is.

- Ask the person who is requesting your time what their deadlines are. If you believe that they are being over-ambitious negotiate a deadline that you know is achievable.

- Balance a willingness to help with what you can realistically achieve in the time available.

In summary, if you have a tendency to over-commit and set yourself unrealistic deadlines, acknowledge it. Yes, other people create time pressures for you but be honest about the self-imposed time pressures. Take the above guidelines on board, as they will help make your days less frantic and less stressful.

CHAPTER 22

Travel and away time

People are travelling more and more on business. The evidence is all around us. The motorways across Europe get busier and busier at peak periods. Air traffic is forecast to increase dramatically over the next twenty years – some of this will be due to increases in leisure travel, but by no means all. Hotels close to business centres are regularly fully booked. As businesses have become more global the people in the businesses have become more mobile. People now regularly fly to meet clients and colleagues within Europe. If you are working for the European subsidiary of an American company you are probably crossing the Atlantic frequently.

Technology can help reduce travel. Rapid communication via the Internet and video conferencing are two examples where technology can in some cases overcome the need for a meeting and therefore the travel involved. However, people will always need to travel to meetings and many of these meetings will involve overnight stays.

Travel is incredibly expensive in time terms. People in a sales role will testify to the frustration of spending six hours driving to attend three customer meetings in a day that totalled three hours. The guidelines provided in Chapter 15 will, I hope, provide some solutions, but there is that inescapable fact that people need to travel to meetings. Overnight stays again impact on time, although again technology helps in that you can always be in contact with base and kept up to date via the e-mail inbox.

The amount of time you spend travelling and away from home will depend on your job role. As stated in the introduction above, all of the evidence is that it is becoming a feature of more and more jobs. For more and more people travel time is taking up more and more time. Is it wasted, totally unproductive time? Certainly if the travel is by car then the answer is probably yes as driving safely requires your full attention! It can of course give you think time and this in itself can be valuable. Accepting that travel and away time is 'time expensive' is there anything you can do to make the most productive use of it? The answer depends on a range of factors – for example, the type of travel and the facilities you have when you are away. There are some general guidelines that can help. As with other topics we have discussed treat the following list as a menu, and select the items that are relevant to your circumstances.

Decide to treat the periods away from home as extended working days

This is a mindset item, which may require you to adopt a new way of working. I am not going back on everything I have said so far about working smarter to reduce your working week! Times away from home lock you out of your family and leisure time. This is inevitable. Therefore make the decision to devote more hours to work when you are away, so that you have time for out of work pursuits when you return.

If you are staying in a city which is new to you, where there are many things of interest to see, you could take the opportunity to use the free time to sightsee. So would I! Where are you staying a lot of the time? In a city you have been to many times before because it is on your business circuit? Staying in a hotel which is similar to many you have stayed in? Where frankly you kick your heels for a couple of nights? Unless you are very lucky you will recognise and be able to relate to these questions. If so, make the most of the free time you have to get ahead of the workload, kill any backlogs that you have. You will get the dividend of more time when you return home.

However, to do this you must be planned and disciplined. The following sections will help you in this.

Plan ahead and make sure you take everything you will need

How many times have you been in a hotel with an empty evening ahead of you? You could spend a couple of hours on a project you have to complete soon. The problem is that you do not have the project files with you. Most of us most of the time are efficient in taking the work with us that is directly related to the meetings we are going to have on the trip. It is worth spending a few moments to think about any free time you may have, what work you may be able to, and make sure that you take the necessary information with you. There is no longer the excuse of the need to travel light – simply download the relevant files from your office-based PC to your laptop.

Use the evenings to sweep up actions left over from the day

We all know that meetings generate follow-on actions and accountabilities. If they do not, then you have to question the validity of the meeting in the first place! The temptation is, after a day of meetings, to get back to the hotel, unwind and decide to write up the meeting reports and action lists when you get back to base.

Now, I do not know about you, but I find that after, say, three days worth of meetings, they can merge into one, so writing up the action points when I get back home can be difficult. Why not make best use of time, and capture the actions and the sweep-up points as you go? Spend an hour or so back at the hotel writing up the necessary reports, follow-on correspondence etc. Incidentally there is an additional benefit. Once you have closed the loop on the day's meetings and logged the follow-up actions in your time system, you can relax. Tomorrow you can focus on the meetings for that day, without the niggling concerns about remembering all of the action points from yesterday's meetings.

Let me reassure you that I am not recommending that you work 24-hour days when you are away. There will be times when you feel the need to 'crash out', go to the hotel gym, go for a drink or have a meal with colleagues. Life is about balance – that's what's important!

Use the benefit of an interrupt free zone

In Chapter 20 we discussed the need to create some interrupt free zones to enable you to focus on specific tasks – for example long-term planning or complex project work. If you are away and travelling alone you have no interrupt time. Colleagues from the office cannot ask for your time and the crises back at the office will have to be resolved without you. Take the opportunity to make some progress on the tasks you find difficult to get time for when you are in the office.

However, I can imagine what you may be thinking – there is no interruption free time, as people can reach me on my mobile phone, they can e-mail me. This is true, and is the flip-side of the communication benefits that technology provides. There is no automatic answer to this problem, but remember the guidelines I provided in Chapter 17 where we covered the e-world issues. Go back to one of the fundamentals of effective time management – prioritise based on importance. If the urgent message on your mobile assumes a greater importance than the project work you were going spend some time on then the usual rules apply: he unplanned can take priority over the planned.

Summary

In summary, planning ahead will enable you to make the most of the 'free time' that you have when you are away. You can make the decision to put in more time when you are away and get the time back when you return.

CHAPTER 23

Be creative as well as corrective

Throughout the previous chapters there has been a recurrent theme – the impact that the unplanned and the crises have on our well thought-out plans. We established at the outset that our time management would be much easier if our worlds were totally predictable. I hope that I have provided you with some practical guidelines to help you manage your unplanned tasks more effectively.

Throughout, there has been acceptance that these unplanned tasks and crises are a given, that we must resign ourselves to the fact that they will always be there. I am not being a defeatist when I say that they are there, that you have to live with them and you have to manage them. However, is there anything you can do to reduce the level of the unplanned? Ask yourself the following questions:

- To what extent are the unscheduled tasks that hit my desk recurring?

- Are there some common causes that generate the crises?

- Can I take some actions to eliminate or at least reduce the level of them?

The answers you come back with are unlikely to be definitive yes or no responses. There will be some crises that happen only once while some unscheduled tasks you must continue to live with. However, I believe that most of us have the opportunity to reduce the levels of crisis and the unplanned.

In the middle of a busy day when we encounter a problem that must be resolved or a task that must be completed we simply do it. We take immediate action, and then return to what we were doing. This is what I call *corrective* action. It is expedient, it is practical, it is the right thing to do – assuming of course that it was a high-priority action that could not have been scheduled for later or possibly delegated. We expect such problems to occur and acknowledge that they go with the territory of the job.

Creative action, however, involves stepping back and asking these questions:

- Why did it happen?

- Is there anything I can do to prevent it happening in the future?

In the chaos and often manic activity of the working day you are unlikely to do this – you will probably be pleased simply to have managed the issue before it escalated to become even more serious! You need some reflection time, to step back. Look back over, say, the last week and study the time stealers, the things that happened that were not scheduled, the things that took you away from your plans. Then ask yourself why they happened, look for the causes.

To understand the causes you may have to talk to members of your team or colleagues in other areas. Once you understand the causes you can then consider what solutions there may be. These may be simple or complex, and you will have to prioritise and use judgement. You may decide that the time it takes to solve the problem is small compared to the time it would take to address the cause. On the other hand, you may find that it will take only a small amount of time to eradicate a problem that involves you in lots of time on an ongoing basis. Or you may even conclude that there is no solution! The important point is that you have stepped back and looked at the opportunities to take creative action.

We come back to some of the fundamental principles that we have discussed before. It is a mindset item. You will need to question and challenge rather than accept and, yes, this will take time. But the investment of time required to analyse the cause and arrive at a solution will give you a payback in the future. Finally, if all you do is take corrective action then nothing will change. The same issues will occur in the future, stealing your time, taking you away from your planned priorities. It is only when you take creative action, take a decision to change something, that you have the opportunity to make inroads into reducing the level of unscheduled tasks and crises.

CHAPTER 24

Managing stress

There are many causes of stress. As this is not a book on stress management I will be restricting the contents of this chapter to stress caused by time – or more often lack of it. There is an old saying that hard work never killed anybody. This is true to some extent; in fact completing a heavy workload or managing a complex task successfully can be rewarding and motivational and give a sense of achievement.

People feel stressed when they have the feeling that they are not in control of events, a feeling they are being driven, not doing the driving. This feeling of being out of control is due to a number of factors:

- There are simply too many things to do in the time available. Where do you start?

- You have not completed one task that you had planned for the day. How can you fit these actions in tomorrow's schedule, which already looks overloaded?

- Everybody is putting demands on your time, all requesting action now. How can you please everybody?

- The priorities keep changing, so all of the planning assumptions of yesterday are wrong. How much extra work are these changes going to cause?

- The only way you can complete everything is to work late again or work over the weekend. How do you tell the family that the planned weekend away will have to be postponed?

I could continue with the list, but I am sure that you can already relate to some of the feelings expressed above. These feelings of stress are understandable and are real. In the introduction I made the point that stress is now recognised by businesses as being a reason for real concern. It affects people's health, reduces their effectiveness and impacts on their private lives. Being able to cope with stress is important – and not just in terms of ensuring that people are more effective. It is important in the context of achieving a work–life balance.

I have stated on a number of occasions that there are no magic answers, no magic wands. In previous chapters we have discussed a number of topics – some relating to mindset, others to specific techniques – that can help you to manage time, to stay in control and therefore to manage stress. In the following guidelines I will be reiterating a number of them in the context of helping you to reduce stress.

First, however, let me repeat a point I have made before. Do not feel that you should take action on all of them. As with previous lists I have suggested that you treat the individual items as a menu. I suggest you decide on your top five – the five most relevant for you, the five that will help you deal with stress more effectively.

Twenty tips for reducing stress

1. *Keep your goals firmly in mind.* If we lose sight of our goals we lose sight of our purpose, the destination we are aiming for. The risk is that we become driven by events and at the extreme our activities become aimless. We feel not in control. This causes stress. When you feel like this stop and remind yourself of your goals to regain our focus. You may have to re-plot your route, but if the goals are still valid stay with them.

2. *Take your goals down to a weekly level.* At the start of each week ask yourself which of your key goals you are going to contribute to. This helps break down a long-term goal into smaller parts and gives you a sense of purpose for the week.

3. *Start each day with your planned actions in place.* Yes, these plans may be overridden but you are starting the day in

control, with a clear sense of what tasks you are going to action. This provides a feeling that you are driving events, not being driven by them. The moment you feel that it is not worth having your plans in place because they will never be realised you are doomed. You are doomed because you will have accepted that you have little or no control.

4. *When in overload respond rather than react.* Reaction is a sense of panic. The workload keeps increasing, so the inclination is to try and work though it blindly, with little hope of succeeding. Response is stepping back – having a coffee, looking at the tasks, assessing the priorities and deciding what you will focus on. It is a realisation that considered response is more effective than manic activity.

5. *Avoid rigid plans.* Being planned is key, but have a plan that is sufficiently flexible to enable you to respond to the unscheduled tasks that you will have to manage. An overly planned day will not give you that flexibility. This is also a mindset item, about learning to live with unexpected. This does not mean that you abandon your plans and priorities. It means that you do not 'fight' the interruptions as a point of principle and attempt to defend your plans no matter what. It is about balancing focus with flex.

6. *Accept that human beings do not work at 100%.* We need breaks, we need time to take stock, to relax. If you have just taken a coffee break and had a social chat with a colleague

do not feel bad or guilty. We are not machines. Taking even short breaks can be therapeutic. However, this is not a licence to be lazy – it is about striking a balance.

7. *Reward yourself for achievement.* Many people are their own severest critics. At the end of the day, reviewing what was achieved, many people focus on what they did not complete and where the plans went wrong. Of course we have to do this so that we can re-schedule the jobs that were not completed. A feeling of failure causes stress. So, in reviewing the day, congratulate yourself for the things that did go well and for the tasks you did complete.

8. *Negotiate on unrealistic deadlines.* Accepting deadlines people give us, regardless of how unrealistic some may be, is initially the easy option. It prevents any conflict, but it causes two problems. The first we have already discussed – you are left with too much work and not enough time. This in itself causes stress. But there is an additional point. You start to feel angry with yourself for not questioning the deadline, for not standing up and negotiating; you then start to resent the person who has made the demand. This causes more stress. Finally, do not feel guilty about not being able to meet the requested deadline. You have a right to defend your priorities and to keep your workload to a reasonable level.

9. *Be a realistic time estimator.* As we have said before we create our own pressures. We commit to actions and completion times without always thinking through the practicalities. Again, do not feel guilty when you say that you cannot action something until tomorrow or the next day. Stress is caused when you over-commit and then find that you cannot deliver.

10. *Avoid sidetracks.* Sidetracks – unless they are valid in that they have a legitimate priority – will result in you losing focus. You will not achieve what you set out to achieve. As I have said, a sense of not achieving can cause stress. Feelings of guilt can also cause stress. Do not feel guilty if you are saying 'no' to people. You are not saying, 'no'. You are saying 'not now'.

11. *Agree some simple codes of practice with colleagues.* Agree some ways of working with your team colleagues, for example to use the ABC–123 priority system. Using a common language can reduce conflicts and misunderstandings, therefore preventing stressful exchanges.

12. *Do not fall into the activity trap.* We are conditioned to seeing hard work as a virtue, as moral. Good citizens are hard workers! While I am not condoning a lazy attitude, there is a difference between hard work and effectiveness. You are being paid to be effective, to deliver results, not to work excessive hours under stress.

13. *Create a sense of achievement by completing tasks and avoid 'multi-tasking'.* Achievement is rewarding, it makes us feel good about ourselves. The point has already been established that generally human beings are not good at multi-tasking. The danger with multi-tasking is that we lose focus and have difficulty in completing any one action. Wherever possible focus on one task at a time and complete it before moving on to the next. Completion is rewarding, but a feeling of having left a number of loose ends can cause stress.

14. *Develop assertive behaviour.* Staying focused involves discussion, dialogue and negotiation. Aggressive behaviour will generate conflict and will therefore lead to stressful situations. Non-assertion will avoid conflict but will cause you to feel frustrated with yourself. Applying assertive behaviour, however, will enable you to protect your priorities, to stay focused and to manage relationships.

15. *Make your self feel good – 'blitz a backlog'.* Routine tasks and items can back up on us. This could be the 320 unanswered e-mails, the mountain of filing, or a range of other administrative tasks. They may not be important as such, but you know that the pile is building. These outstanding tasks can cause stress. Take action to kill the backlog. Allocate half a day, steel yourself, and work through until the backlog has gone. You may not have

enjoyed the task, but the relief of it not being there anymore will make you feel good.

16. *Go for some early wins during the day.* If you can cross a key task off your list early in the day it will help you to feel good about yourself! The remainder of the day may become chaotic, with many of your scheduled tasks being replaced with some crisis management. If you can remind yourself that the 'big task' has already been completed you will feel better. You will feel a sense of achievement, enabling you to put the not so good parts of the day into perspective.

17. *If you are getting overloaded acknowledge it.* If you are reaching overload and getting into backlog acknowledge it to yourself and to a colleague or your boss. It is not a sin and there is no need to hide it or to feel guilty! Just talking to someone can help. Discuss what can be rescheduled, what can be delegated. It is not an easy option – saying 'I need help' takes confidence. However, being a hero and trying to battle through on your own is not helpful to you or others.

18. *Protect your out of work time.* This is crucial. There are always reasons, given a busy schedule, to put in more hours, to sacrifice the other parts of your life. Protecting your free time is beneficial to you, your family and your employer. A stressed person will not be effective.

19. *Attack the top time stealers.* Feeling out of control, as I have said, causes stress. Taking decisive action puts you in control. Identify the top five time stealers and put in place a 30-day plan to find solutions to minimise or eradicate them. In the last chapter we looked at creative action as opposed to corrective action. Creative action involves stepping back to analyse the causes of time stealers. Use this approach in your 30-day plan.

20. *Focus on facts not on feelings.* In a situation where people are putting demand upon demand on you emotion can creep in. At the extreme you can feel a victim! Objectivity is lost and you may overreact to requests. Assertion is replaced with aggression. This in turn causes conflict, which can lead to stress. Step back – attack the time problem not the person. It is unlikely that there is a plot to overload you with work!

Summary

It may be that simply adopting one of the twenty tips above will eliminate the stresses you are under caused by time pressures. However, it is more likely that a combination of, say, four or five will be needed. Before you leave this chapter briefly re read the twenty tips, and identify your own top five – the five that you believe will help you the most. Make a note of them in the spaces provided on the next page.

Top five tips for managing stress

1.
2.
3.
4.
5.

PART 5

Specific time management techniques – key messages and action plan

Be in tune with your body

- Establish when your high and low energy periods are – this is your energy curve.

- Schedule complex and demanding tasks for action during your periods of high energy.

- Leave the routine/maintenance tasks for low energy periods.

- Remember that your energy levels at the mental and physical levels are different. Physical exercise can influence and improve your energy levels back at work.

Delegating

- Delegating is not just about delegating tasks to subordinates. You can delegate to team members, peers – even your boss.

- Do not confuse delegation with abdication.

- Effective delegation not only provides time management opportunities – it can be motivational and give people development opportunities.

- Analyse your tasks in terms of must do, should do, could do, should not do and where cover is needed. This will highlight where the delegation possibilities are.

Meetings

- Meetings are necessary – they are an important part of business and essential for building relationships. However, they are significant time stealers.

- Ask if a meeting is really necessary. Consider the options. Technology increases the number of options.

- Before deciding on a meeting count the cost.

- If you decide that a meeting is necessary take steps to ensure that it is effective. Have a clear goal and agenda, impose a time limit to focus people's minds, capture the commitments, summarise, confirm and follow up to ensure that the agreed actions are taken.

Think 'team'

- Time management is not just a personal development item.

- We have an impact on others, and people have an impact on us and on our time.

- Discuss and agree some time management practices with your team and other close colleagues.

- Agree a team language and a shared time management code.

The e-world issues

- Use technology intelligently.

- Action e-mails as you would a paper in-tray.

- Do not become a compulsive e-mail checker.

- Learn to live with the pace of the e-world. This will require you to balance focus with flexibility.

- Home-based working requires even more discipline if you are going to be an effective time manager.

- Grab the opportunities home working provides to make the most effective use of time and to achieve a better work–life balance.

- Be aware of the danger of extending your working day because the office is only a few yards away.

Be decisive – go for the hard tasks

- We all have tasks that we would really prefer not to do. Putting them off is not the answer.
- Indecision is in itself a time stealer.
- Prioritise on a rational basis, not on your personal preferences.
- Break down daunting tasks into manageable bites.
- Choose a high energy period to work on them.

Task batching

- Most people are not good at multi-tasking.
- Wherever possible finish one task before you move on to the next.
- Batch tasks of the same type and action them *en bloc*. You will be quicker, more time effective.

No interrupt zones

- Allocate windows of time as interruption free.

- Schedule them for times of the day when your general workload is usually at its lowest level in relative terms.

- Agree these time slots with your colleagues.

- Use this time to work on complex tasks that require concentration. Focus on the 'future' tasks.

Realistic time estimation

- We create some of our own time pressures.

- Think before you offer a deadline for completing a task.

- Check what is acceptable to the person making the request.

- Avoid over-committing and under-performing.

Travel and away time

- Plan ahead. Think of the tasks you can be working on when you have 'free time' away on business.

- Ensure that you take all of the records and information with you that you will need to complete those tasks.

- Consider extended hours when working away from home. Take the opportunity to make inroads into any backlog of work. You will get the time back when you return home.

- Sweep up actions left over from the day when you return to the hotel. Again this will save you time when you return to the office.

- Use the benefit of interruption-free time.

Be creative as well as corrective

- Identify the recurring time stealers.

- Do not stop at handling the problem or managing the crisis.

- Ask yourself what are the causes of the problems that take up your time.

- Take creative action to eliminate them in the future or to reduce their frequency.

Managing stress

- There are a number of causes of stress. Time pressure is one of them.

- Stress impacts on your life and makes you less effective at work

- Select the most relevant suggestions from the twenty tips given in Chapter 24 for reducing stress caused by time pressures. Apply these and assess how they help you.

Part 5

Points for action

What have been the major learning points from this part of the book?
1.
2.
3.
4.
5.

What specific actions do you intend to take to develop your time management effectiveness? Select no more than *five* actions and list in priority sequence. Prioritise based on the positive impact you believe the action will have. Commit to timescales – when you intend to implement the action.
1.
2.
3.
4.
5.

PART 6

The beginning

CHAPTER 25

Where do you go from here?

In my role as a training consultant I have facilitated numerous programmes on time management and other leadership and management topics. A programme may last for a year, and involve a number of workshops, web-based learning and work-based projects. At the other extreme a programme may consist of just one workshop on a highly focused topic, such as time management.

Understandably, when reaching the end of a programme the participants have the feeling of we have finished, we have completed the programme. A key message that I always try and leave people with is that this is not the finishing line, this is the starting point. The company has invested money in the programme. The participants have invested their time. The payback on that investment is only realised if what has been learned is applied back in the workplace.

Reading a book such as this is a self-directed learning exercise. It is similar to a training course in the sense that your objective is to develop your skills, knowledge and competence. What have you invested so far? In financial terms you have invested in the price of the book. Your investment in time terms is the time that it has taken you to read it. So, you are already applying one of the key principles of effective time management by investing time to make time. If, however, having completed the book, you put it down, and change nothing in your time management practices, then you will receive no payback. You will have invested with no return.

At the end of each part I have encouraged you to list the five key actions that you intend to take, actions that you believe will be the most helpful in developing your time effectiveness. Given that you have completed the core five parts of the book you will have logged up to 25 specific action points. This is a good starting point. You may have already put some of these in to place. The question now is how do you keep the momentum going?

Let me briefly review what I believe are the *essential* items for you to 'sign up to' as prerequisites for developing your time effectiveness. I will provide you with some guidelines to help you put your own time management development plan in place.

The essential six 'sign-up' factors

1. Go back to the 'Ten Commandments' of effective time management. These are the mindset items, the underlying

values and principles that support the practice of effective time management. Keep these firmly in your focus. Introducing specific time management techniques and making them work for you will be much easier if you have bought into these core principles.

2. Be clear about your *goals*. Remember that the goals are your destination. Completing tasks and actions are the means of progressing down the road. Goals provide the direction and define your priority actions.

3. Probably the most important time management skill is the ability to *prioritise*, to make the right decisions about what to do and what not to do when those choices have to be made. Always remember the primary decision should be based on importance not deadlines.

4. The first three points are primarily about *getting focused*. Once focused you need to *be organised*. Having a system or a process is a prerequisite for getting and staying organised. If you do not already use some form of time system I strongly urge you to invest in one – the investment will be repaid many times over. The system need not be complex. In fact the easier to use and update the better.

5. Investing in a system in itself will not give you a payback. *Discipline is needed* – the discipline to keep the system current, and the discipline of investing ten minutes each day

to review the day, adjust your priorities as necessary and plan the next day.

6. *Staying focused* requires a different set of skills. These are the behavioural skills to help you negotiate deadlines, manage interruptions, hold on to your priorities –be tough on time, not on the people.

Putting your own development plan in place

Before you put this book down and consign it to the coffee table or the bookcase, *invest up to 30 minutes of your time now*. Work through the following tasks:

- Define your work and out of work priority goals for the next six months, if you have not already done so.
- List down the key tasks and actions that you will need to take to achieve those goals.
- Prioritise the 25 possible actions that you have logged so far – you will remember you were asked to list out five at the end of each part. Select five that you intend to focus on in the next two months.
- Commit to review these plans at the end of each month, at least for the next three months.
- Put all of the above commitments into your time system, or diary if you do not yet have a time system.

One last thing . . .

Finally, managing time is not a perfect science as there are too many variables. I started by stating that there is no single solution for *taming time*. The combined effects of a number of different actions and applying a range of techniques will make a difference. My objective has been to provide you with the essentials to enable you to develop your time effectiveness. I hope that this objective has been achieved.